MARTY LIQUORI'S GUIDE FOR THE ELITE RUNNER

OTHER BOOKS BY MARTY LIQUORI

On the Run (with Skip Myslenski)

OTHER BOOKS BY JOHN L. PARKER, JR.

The Frank Shorter Story

Once a Runner

Runners and Other Ghosts on the Trail

MARTY LIQUORI'S GUIDE FOR THE ELITE RUNNER

Marty Liquori
and John L. Parker, Jr.

A Playboy Press Book

First Edition

Library of Congress Cataloging in Publication Data

Liquori, Marty.
Marty Liquori's guide for the elite runner.

1. Running. I. Parker, John L., Jr., joint author.
II. Playboy. III. Title.
GV1061.L567 796.4'26 80-7728
ISBN 0-87223-625-0

Designed by Tere LoPrete

The charts on pp. 13, 14, 22, and 23 are reprinted from *A Scientific Approach to Distance Running* by David Costill by permission of Tafnew's Press.

To Carol, who is always at the finish line.

—MARTY LIQUORI

This book is for my late father, John L. Parker, Sr., my mother, Florence, and for someone named Mary Ann.

—JOHN L. PARKER, JR.

CONTENTS

MARTY LIQUORI'S GUIDE FOR THE ELITE RUNNER

INTRODUCTION

There are many books now on the market, some relatively good, some very lamentable, which propose to advise the novice runner on such esoterica as the proper lacing of running shoes or the most effective method of discouraging territorially minded canines.

Indeed, with all the writing going on about running these days, it is somewhat ironic that the only group consistently unheard from is the elite runners themselves.

What is an elite runner? You might be surprised to find out that the fellow from two streets over who wins his age group practically every time out is nowhere close to elite. Our admittedly subjective chart on page 116 defines an elite runner as someone who can run a mile under 4:10, 10,000 meters under 31:00, or a marathon under 2:23.

Those are pretty tough requirements, but then again the stopwatch has always been a coldly objective judge of an athlete's ability. That has traditionally been the allure of the footrace: No amount of charm or politicking will improve your performance by so much as a second.

And that brings us to a rather touchy point: most of the "experts" that runners have been going to for advice lately would barely qualify as Category B or C runners under our definitions (they run a mile between 5:00 and 6:00). That is not to say that one must be a champion runner to write accurately and persuasively about the subject of distance running. Indeed, some of the historic coaching figures in this sport have been mediocre or poor runners themselves.

The point is simply that in order to be taken seriously as an "authority" on distance running, one probably ought to boast more meaningful qualifications than (1) having "completed" several marathons and (2) owning a typewriter.

But then again this book was not written for everyone who calls himself or herself a "runner." It was written for the athlete who, regardless of age, sex, or motivation, wants to dispense with the excuses and alibis and to compete *seriously* at this most difficult sport.

If the reader is that runner, or thinks he or she is that runner, this book ought to become your constant companion for a long time.

FOREWORD

In elucidating the concepts expressed in this book, we have tried to ground our conclusions wherever possible on the scholarship and scientific methodology of respected researchers in physiology and related fields, and to give proper credit for their work in the appropriate places.

We are particularly indebted to Dr. David Costill of Ball State University, who is perhaps the premier exercise physiologist in the United States, for his *A Scientific Approach to Distance Running* (Tafnews Press, 1979).

As any casual observer of modern distance-running training knows, all current runners owe a great deal to the outstanding New Zealand coach Arthur Lydiard, and the reader will be able easily to tell how much the training methods in this book are a reflection of his genius, as well as that of my own college coach, the renowned Jumbo Elliot of Villanova University.

It is not at all easy to become a successful distance runner;

successful, that is, in terms of winning or competing well in races.

It requires, very simply, living a life that few are prepared to live. And to live it for long periods of time, several years perhaps, before genuine results can be expected.

Therein lies the difference between the romantic perception and the all-too-dreary reality. It is the difference between looking at the Sistine Chapel ceiling and lying flat on one's back for a number of years doing highly intricate, soul-consuming work. It is the pigment dropping back into one's eyes that gets lost in the translation.

The decision to undertake a project like serious distance running should be the occasion for considerable informed introspection, which is precisely why I begin this book with a chapter on making "the Decision." Pray do not pass it by in your haste to get to meatier things. In doing so, you might well miss the most important personal consideration in serious running: whether to do it at all.

But beyond that, the remainder of the book is an attempt to digest all the currently available scientific knowledge, to absorb the myriad charts and graphs, to apply a very practical runner's sensibilities and experiences to them, and then to put that information in words that will both please and enlighten.

One final note: To those marathoners or ultramarathoners who might be loath to take advice from "mere" milers or 5,000-meter men, I hasten to point out that successful training programs for both the mile and the marathon these days are far more similiar than dissimilar. I have trained often with either half-milers or marathoners without any great trauma.

Further (by way of empirical data that all runners can grasp), without any specialized preparation or tricked-up training, most good track distance runners would have little difficulty in jumping into marathon races and running under 2:25 or so.

It is through a basic understanding of the physiology of

training that improvement comes to the distance runner, whether half-miler or marathoner. No coach is wise enough to be able to prescribe the exact right workout to a runner every day of the year. For this reason, the runner must necessarily become a uniquely self-reliant athlete.

Chapter One

The Decision

I beg you take a moment here.

The absolutely essential first step toward becoming a competitive runner, at no matter what level, is to decide if you truly want to do it.

Easy enough, you say. Since I have the book in my hand, obviously I'm interested in pursuing this thing. Let's get on with it.

But the decision to undergo serious training should never be taken lightly. No one knows better than those who have been at the top of the heap. For them, the aching questions "One more race? One more season?" are not in the least rhetorical.

A commitment to serious training means that no matter what else you are in this world—doctor, lawyer, Indian chief—first of all you are a runner. If you are unable to live up to that standard, your running is not truly "serious" and you can expect your race results to show it.

Running and other endurance sports are the most unforgiving of mistresses. You can drop out of law school for a year and come back to it later, picking up where you left off. Few things, certainly not knowledge, fade as quickly as the results of hard physical training. It is a flower that does not last long past the picking.

Training therefore must be constant. The first day you miss training, you begin a backward slide. You cannot pick up where you left off, since you have already slid several feet back down the mountain. You cannot put your body on hold; in distance running you are either getting better or getting worse at any given moment. There is no status quo in the world of the distance runner.

Which is not to say that you must undertake, as some of the literature would have you believe, absurdly ascetic and eccentric life-styles. You needn't ponder the prospects of dining on nuts and berries. You won't have to absolutely forsake drinking, late nights, carousing in general.

What you will have to do is train. And train hard. Whatever else you can fit into your life after that is your own business.

Before you undertake that "final" decision, consider some of these ponderables:

TALENT: DO YOU HAVE THE PLUMBING?

It sounds strange to hear good runners talking about "talent."

"Oh, so and so had a lot of talent . . ." someone will say, usually in reference to how "so and so" managed to squander same.

But the term, when measured against its use in other sports, is very appropriate. "Talent" is simply that which God (or whatever entity or good fortune you choose to believe in) gives you at birth. With distance runners "talent" is "plumbing," i.e., the heart, lungs, and circulatory system, and the muscles that rely on them. In short, it is the equipment needed to transport and burn oxygen and fuel in order to cover ground. That is a pretty fair basic definition of the physical act of running; all that remains is to point out that some people are just naturally better at it than others.

That is apparently painful to accept for some.

We all know that it takes particular innate qualities to become a championship quarterback. We all accept the fact that not everyone can do it. But for some reason, many insist that the world of the competitive runner be more egalitarian.

There is perhaps no one truism of distance running more misunderstood than this: We all bring our own genetic pluses and minuses to the starting line with us.

Given time and effort, almost anyone can cover relatively long distances. Almost anyone can show remarkable improvement through training. It is a seductive proposition indeed: Success in distance running depends solely on dedication and hard work.

It becomes, alas, a bitter pill for the new competitive runner finally to come to realize that we are not, in fact, all born equal with regard to our ability to cover ground quickly on foot.

All this will be discussed later in more detail. For the time being, the reader should be aware that as far as running potential goes, there are those among us more blessed than others.

Also be aware of the very understandable human reluctance to admit that this is true. (We all apparently want to think there is one field in which hard work and *nothing* else pays off.)

One telling example of such understandable bias comes from an otherwise primly scientific book; it should illustrate the current disdain for the noxious realities of an unfair universe: "Some well-conditioned runners will beat less conditioned yet better endowed runners. *Unfortunately*, the reverse will often be true."[1] (emphasis added)

Perhaps in no other sport is natural "talent" less admired than in distance running.

At the top level, it hardly matters. To do well competitively in those circles, absolute dedication is a prerequisite no matter what kind of lungs mom and dad bequeathed you.

At a more mundane competitive level, however, it is still possible to make up for considerable genetic shortcomings by plain hard work.

The two controlling factors we are all, for better or worse, stuck with are: (1) our oxygen uptake rate (VO_2), which is nothing more than our ability to utilize oxygen in the creation of energy (see figure 1), and (2) the proportion of "slow-twitch" to "fast-twitch" fibers in our muscle composition (see figure 2).

Oxygen uptake can be improved to a distinctly limited extent by training. Likewise, the proportion of slow-twitch to fast-twitch muscles is not subject to alteration in this life.

As will be discussed later, these matters are subject to scientific measurement, and it might be advisable for the new competitive runner to know ahead of time whether he or she has been endowed with the kind of physical equipment which will allow for world-class performances somewhere down the road. It might not be the sort of thing to base your whole running future on, but it would be helpful in setting realistic goals.

There are several clinics in the United States that do research in this area, the most notable being Dr. David Costill's Human Performance Laboratory at Ball State University, in Muncie, Indiana.

The runner who is truly curious about his or her long-range potential as a competitive athlete might contact one of them and inquire about the possibility of testing.

No matter what the results, however, the runner should

Figure 1

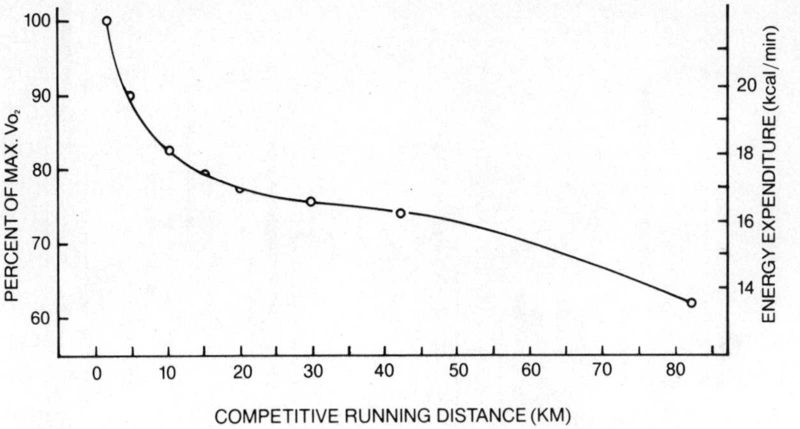

PERCENTAGE OF THE RUNNER'S MAXIMAL OXYGEN UPTAKE UTILIZED DURING COMPETITION IN RACES OF VARIED DISTANCES

From *A Scientific Approach to Distance Running* by David Costill (Los Altos: Tafnews Press,1979).

Figure 2

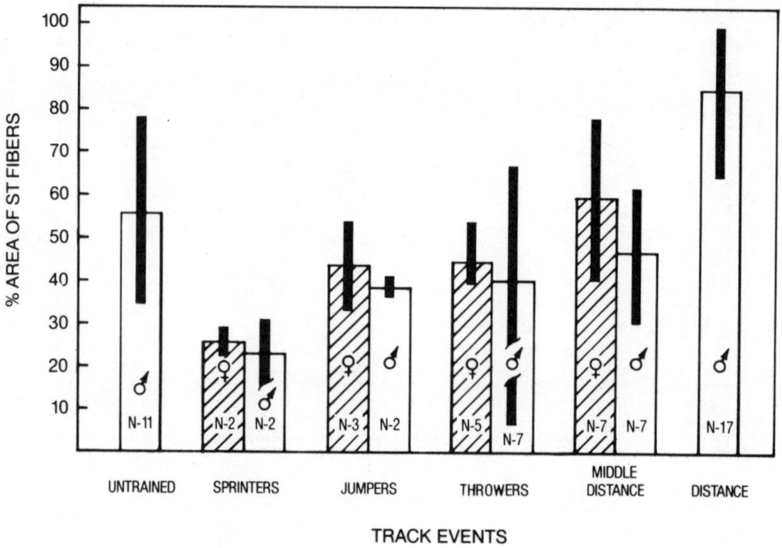

PERCENTAGE OF GASTROCNEMIUS MUSCLE AREA COMPOSED OF SLOW-TWITCH FIBERS IN UNTRAINED MEN AND TRAINED TRACK ATHLETES

From *A Scientific Approach to Distance Running* by David Costill (Los Altos: Tafnews Press,1979).

never be giddily encouraged or abjectly discouraged by them. Athletic history has taught us time and time again that when two human beings compete against each other, the most important factor is not the body but the mind.

Chapter Two

The Science

It has taken many years for the scientists with their test tubes and centrifuges to catch up with what good runners and their coaches have long known from listening attentively to the body's own voices.

In a few instances, the medical world's complete lack of experience with highly trained athletes has led to confusion and unnecessary personal turmoil. One example should suffice to make the point: Australian Kerry O'Brien, a former world-record-holding steeplechaser (a grueling two-mile race over hurdles and a water jump) produced an abnormal electrocardiogram and was told it would be dangerous for him to continue his sport.

Several years later, after many more world-class athletes had been tested on the machine, it was discovered that a large proportion of all elite runners produced graphs which, in a clinical setting, would be cause for alarm.[2]

Scientists and doctors still do not know *why* highly conditioned hearts dance to such mysterious and unseen orchestras, but they have at long last determined something that anyone who ever raced against Mr. O'Brien could have told them with no sense of irony whatsoever: The gentleman is *not* sick.

As medical researchers and exercise physiologists learn more about the science of exercise, it becomes increasingly clear that upper-echelon runners and coaches have been light-years ahead of the scientists in determining how to develop endurance in the human animal. But while the latest scientific findings have been of little help in fashioning new training techniques, they have provided after-the-fact explanations as to why certain training philosophies and practices (most particularly those of New Zealand's Arthur Lydiard) have been more successful than others.

With that in mind, we undertake a quick tour of the current scientific knowledge as it relates to competitive distance running.

A TWITCH IN TIME

Although there is some disagreement as to whether this is an oversimplification, most exercise physiologists agree that muscle fiber may be divided into two broad categories, "slow twitch" (ST) and "fast twitch" (FT).

The slow muscle cells contract with less force but are more efficient for long-duration work. Each slow cell contains a high proportion of mitochondria, the tiny "energy factories" where fuel is burned with oxygen to create energy and the by-products, carbon dioxide and water, both of which are easily disposed by the bloodstream.

The reason the ST fibers, which have a high oxygen content, are more efficient is that when FT cells create energy *without oxygen* through an entirely different process, the debilitating by-product lactic acid is formed, and the cells have greater difficulty disposing of it. Lactic acid is the prime cause of fatigue in the shorter distance races (10,000 meters and under).

Just to complicate things a little further, scientists have now found there is an FT muscle cell which is *also* highly oxidative, like the ST cells. To distinguish them, they call the oxidative FT fiber "fast twitch red" and the nonoxidative FT fiber "fast twitch white." It is helpful to think of the distinction this way: The fast-twitch white cells produce the sudden, explosive energy needed by a sprinter in a 100-yard dash, whereas the fast-twitch red cells can be thought of as a half-miler or miler's type muscles, producing the long, flowing semisprint needed to run a mile in four minutes or a half-mile in 1:48. Thus, there are actually three general muscle cell types: slow-twitch red, fast-twitch red, and fast-twitch white.

In any race that lasts more than a few yards, energy will be provided by a constant interplay of all three muscle cell types. In order to understand the training techniques that follow, it is important to have a working knowledge of each cell type and how it produces energy.

Attempts to correlate laboratory findings with practical competitive results are at times confusing, but there can be little doubt that successful distance runners generally have a high percentage of ST muscle, whereas sprinters and jumpers have a predictably high proportion of FT fibers.

In one test in which a muscle biopsy was performed on twenty elite runners in 1972, the average percentage of the body's ST fibers was 79, and several were much higher (up to 98).[3]

The proportion of ST to FT-white and FT-red will likely be shown to be one of the controlling factors in forecasting an individual's potential for success, as well as helping to predict the most promising distance at which to seek the olive wreath.

Once again, good coaches and successful athletes have for many years been unknowingly juggling ST-FT considerations when deciding which event a runner might best be suited for. "So and so is too slow in the quarter to run a really good mile, but he has plenty of strength for the three-mile . . ." is the way the layman-coach might have described an athlete's relative abilities.

Whatever new revelations researchers may have in store for us regarding the various muscle fiber types and their respective roles in energy production, one fact should be very clear to the serious runner: Though the heart, lungs, and digestive system are the most visible and obvious components of the body's energy system, the real secrets behind a 2:09 marathon or a four-minute mile are locked inside the membranes of each individual cell.

"THE BEAR" AND "THE WALL"

There are two distinct kinds of fatigue that will slow or stop the runner. They are so different that runners have evolved separate terms for each, terms that imply (with typical runner understatement) the subtle nuances of each.

"The bear," known to any former track man who has been pressed into unfamiliar duty on his team's mile relay squad, is a debilitating buildup of lactic acid in the muscles. The term can be heard in the following context: "Coming out of the last turn I thought I had him all the way. Then the bear jumped on my back."

Comedian Bill Cosby, in a classic rendition of his own experience on his college mile-relay team, had his own description: ". . . and then . . . all of a sudden . . . *Rigor mortis* set in." The condition has also been called "pushing a piano." Whatever one calls it, anyone who has ever been through it knows what it feels like.

The "bear" jumps on a distance runner when he has invaded his anaerobic (i.e., nonoxygen-efficient) energy system by running faster than his aerobic (i.e., oxygen-efficient) system can supply energy for. Thus a miler necessarily finishes a race with plenty of glycogen (a sugar, deposited in muscles, which is a main source of energy) left in his system, but with his legs moving painfully through the mire of his own muscle lactates.

For that reason, most middle-distance runners, knowing they will have to invade that anaerobic system heavily during competition, will spend a good portion of their training time on "interval training," which is nothing more than relatively short, fast runs with a prescribed rest period in between. Such training is calculated to toughen the muscles to faster paces, to groove the anaerobic pathways, and to inure the runner to the handling of a lactic-acid load while performing at maximal levels.

"The wall" is something altogether different, implying as it does some mystical yet very definitive human barrier from which one staggers away dazed and shaken. Which is precisely the case, of course.

Physiologically speaking, "the wall" is the point at which the runner has depleted his glycogen supplies and must either stop or slow down to the point at which remaining trace energy supplies can handle the demand.

Shortly after winning the gold medal in the Munich Olympic marathon, Frank Shorter made the distinction between the two types of fatigue when he spoke of the last three miles of his victorious race: ". . . I pretty much knew that I had it won [at that point] barring a complete breakdown. Right about then, however, your muscles are starting to give out on you. *It's not as if the bear's getting you,* but you can feel yourself slowly sinking. It becomes a matter of time and physics. It is almost beyond your control . . ."[4] (emphasis added)

It is not surprising that Shorter would press the distinction between the two kinds of fatigue on the interviewer. Shorter had himself been primarily a 5,000- and 10,000-meter runner until shortly before the games (as well as a competitor in the mile in college), and so would have been all too familiar with the large furry mammal that lies in ambush on the last turn of every 440-yard oval in trackdom.

In summary, "the bear" refers to a debilitating oxygen debt brought on by heavy reliance on the anaerobic system, whereas "the wall" is a depletion of the absolutely necessary glycogen fuel (see figure 3).

Ultimately, all distance training is geared toward the production of maximum energy while avoiding both bears and walls.

ENERGY: THREE STAGES

During the course of a long race, the runner's body will rely on three different sources of energy, and it will do so in rather distinct phases. One could think of it almost in the same sense that a car has three forward gears, except for the fact that in the body all three are usually engaged at the same time, but with primary emphasis on only one (see figure 4). (In distances longer than the marathon, there are actually *more* than three stages of energy production, but we shall omit those here.)

For the first few seconds of any strenuous activity, the body gets energy from the anaerobic breakdown of muscle glycogen and blood glucose. That oxygen-less system will operate until the slower-starting aerobic system gets warmed up. This is what is commonly referred to as the "second wind." If the demand for energy is great and the time is short, as in a sprint, the anaerobic system will continue operating until it shuts itself off as a result of lactic-acid buildup. This shut-off will occur after about two minutes (about the amount of time it takes a good high school half-miler to complete his event) assuming maximum effort.

If the pace is slow enough, the aerobic system begins to shoulder the burden after a few seconds of anaerobic activity.

Figure 3

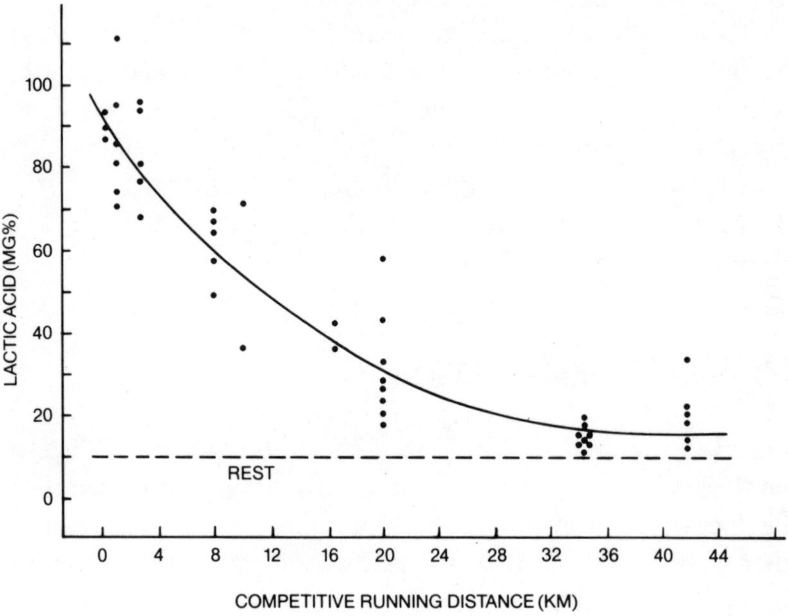

BLOOD-LACTIC-ACID CONCENTRATION AT END OF DISTANCE RACES OF FROM 1.6 TO 42 KM IN LENGTH

From *A Scientific Approach to Distance Running* by David Costill (Los Altos: Tafnews Press,1979).

Figure 4

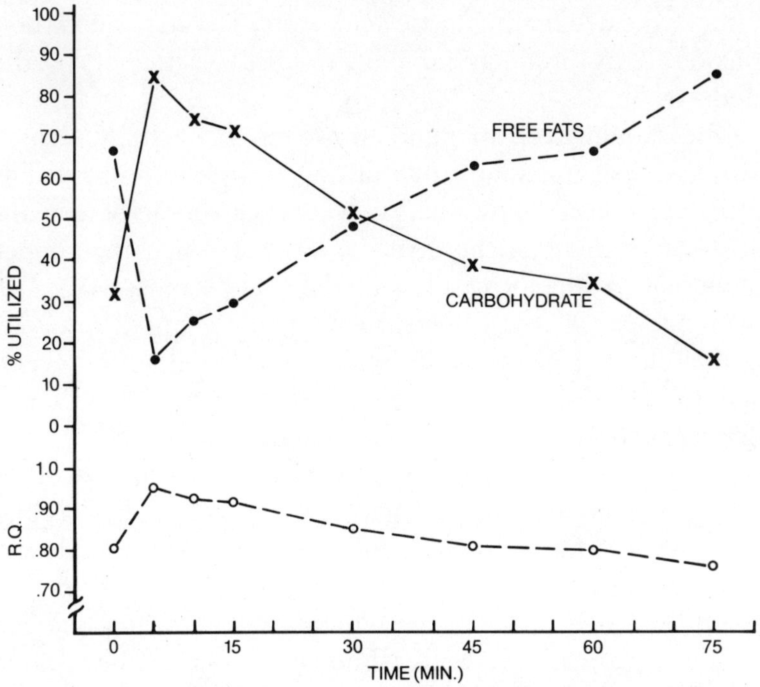

CHANGES IN THE RESPIRATORY EXCHANGE (R.Q.) OF OXYGEN AND CARBON DIOXIDE, INDICATING A SHIFT OF THE UTILIZATION OF CARBOHYDRATES AND FATS BY THE WORKING MUSCLES

From *A Scientific Approach to Distance Running* by David Costill (Los Altos: Tafnews Press,1979).

It works by converting muscle and liver glycogen (carbohydrates) into energy by burning them in the presence of oxygen. This produces an efficient high level of energy without the debilitating lactic acid. Instead, water and carbon dioxide are by-products and both are easily carried off by the bloodstream.

One should keep in mind, however, that the anaerobic pathway does not shut down during this phase, but remains available to contribute energy whenever the aerobic pathways cannot handle the demand, such as when the runner encounters a hill, or a surge in the middle of a race. The price one pays for that instant emergency energy, however, is the old bugaboo, lactic acid, which will take several minutes (and several liters of oxygen) to remove. This is also referred to as going into "oxygen debt."

Every runner knows what oxygen debt feels like. It is the "blown-out" feeling one gets at the top of a hill, a feeling which makes the legs painful and heavy, as if the race should be over already. But after a few moments (sometimes at a greatly reduced pace) the heaviness goes away and one can resume a normal pace again. The runner has simply drawn upon his or her anaerobic system to handle the hill, incurred an oxygen debt because of it, paid it back as his or her bloodstream dispersed the lactic acid, and then gone back to the more comfortable aerobic pace.

Stage Three comes fully into play after about 30 minutes of activity when the body begins to utilize fully yet another fuel in the aerobic system: fat. A highly concentrated fuel, fat requires a bit more oxygen to burn than do carbohydrates, but the process creates no lactic acid.

This fat-burning final stage is very important for racing distances between six and twenty-six miles. Why? Because although fat does not replace glycogen as a fuel during long races, it does serve as an efficient partial substitute, thus forestalling eventual glycogen depletion, which will all but stop the runner.

Glycogen depletion will bring a runner to an ignominious halt even though he or she still has fat reserves. It seems that burning *some* glycogen is necessary even when the body is using mostly fat as fuel. One study of a subject on a treadmill for two hours revealed that during the first ten minutes of running, fats contributed 39 percent of the total fuel, but during the final minutes the figure jumped to 67 percent.[5]

This fat-burning aerobic phase is the reason so many middle-distance runners engage in marathon-type training during at least part of the year. The more the body can be trained to burn fat, the longer it can forestall the depletion of its glycogen. One study has revealed that a gastrocnemius muscle was *seven times* more efficient at burning fat after marathon training than before.[6]

OXYGEN AND THE CELLULAR CONNECTION

"What about breathing?" someone from the audience of a running clinic inevitably asks.

"What about it?" is the equally inevitable response from the guest runner. Or he may be even more flip: "Breathing? I recommend it heartily."

Breathing is something that competitive runners do not lose a great deal of sleep about. The reason beginners and novices find it occupying their minds is they feel sure they aren't doing it right. They're having trouble getting enough air into their bodies. They're getting "winded."

What they are really experiencing is the external symptom of an internal cellular problem. It's not that they can't get enough air, but that their cells can't use the oxygen they *are* getting. The brain interprets this as a lack of oxygen, demands more from the already laboring lungs, and we quickly find the runner panting, "winded."

The answer is not to be found in breathing but in training. There is no substitute for making muscle cells more efficient at burning fuel and oxygen and elminating wastes. The only good advice that can be given about breathing itself is to relax the face muscles (the blank runner's "mask") and to breathe through both the nose and mouth.[7] After that, it's up to your cells.

Although it is generally recognized that long-distance training increases heart size, stroke volume (the amount of blood pumped on each beat), and capillary density, running efficiency finally depends on the muscle cell's ability to use oxygen to burn fuel and eliminate wastes.

How does training affect basic cellular metabolism?

Running long distances has been shown to cause an increase in both the number of mitochondria and the secretion of enzymes around the mitochondria which facilitiate the fuel-burning process. The mitochondria are where it all happens in aerobic energy production.

Research has shown that increases in mitochondrial and enzyme activity within the cell are directly related to the *duration* of training runs.[8] As we will discuss later, this scientifically established fact fits in well with long-established training theories which hold that a "base" of long, relatively slow distance runs should be used to prepare even the half-miler for competitive running.[9] Indeed, there is nothing more *basic* to distance running than beefing up the cell's ability to use oxygen in the mitochondria.

Research has demonstrated that ten minutes of running is necessary to increase an oxidative enzyme by 10 percent in rat muscle, whereas 30 minutes would cause a 30 percent increase, 60 minutes a 40 percent increase, and 120 minutes a 100 percent increase in the same enzyme. But training in excess of 120 minutes was actually counterproductive, leading to exhaustion and the inability to attain even formerly achievable time goals.[10] This finding is in accordance with current training theories which hold that maximum benefits from training are derived by running between 80 and 140 miles per week, and that training in excess of these distances will not likely be beneficial, and could be counterproductive.

Increasing the number and efficiency of the mitochondria is especially important for the longer races because the greater the number of mitochondria, the less each one has to be stimulated to begin burning fat instead of glycogen. In short, the muscle cell arrives at the most efficient third stage of energy production earlier in the run and thus conserves the all-important glycogen for later effort. And in the longer distances (as opposed to the middle distances, where lactic-acid buildup is the limiting factor) it is the depletion of glycogen which slows or stops the competitor.

Whether they put it in scientific terms or not, nearly every knowledgeable coach and runner these days uses long, relatively easy training runs as an early-season base for the overall aerobic conditioning of middle- and long-distance runners. They are merely building up the mitochondrial activity in each cell, preparing for future demands, putting off as long as possible the eventual collision between the runner and the wall.

OXYGEN AND ITS DELIVERY TO THE CELLS

Although the body's most important and fundamental adaptations to distance training take place at the cellular level, the most obvious changes to the observer (whether casual or scientific) involve the enhancement of the oxygen transport system, i.e., the lungs, heart, blood, arteries, capillaries, and veins.

Perhaps the most dramatic transformation of all is that of the heart, whose pulsating walls grow thicker and stronger, and whose overall size increases measurably with training. The late Steve Prefontaine's heart, for instance, was 30 to 40 percent larger than that of a normal adult his size.[11] And it has been reported that the great Paavo Nurmi, the "Flying Finn" of the 1920s, was powered by a heart nearly three times normal size.[12] Once again, experimentation with animals gives confirmation; it has been shown that rats experience measurable cardiac enlargement with as little as ten minutes daily training.[13]

Although an enlarged heart would be cause for alarm in a clinical setting, it is quite normal among runners. The heart is, after all, perhaps more innately suited to distance running than any other group of muscle fibers in the body. It is composed entirely of slow-twitch, highly oxidative muscle fiber, and even in an untrained state has an extremely high mitochondrial content and a dense system of blood vessels. One way of looking at it is to consider that the heart is the one muscle that is *always* doing aerobic work, even when the body is at rest. Since it has probably already achieved, in an untrained state, its most efficient cellular adaptation through Darwinian evolution (in other words, the heart can*not* increase its mitochondrial activity through training), the only avenue left for adaptation to the increased demands of distance running is simply to grow larger and stronger.

The trained heart does this so well that it beats less often, at rest *or* during exercise, than the same untrained heart, while actually increasing the amount of blood pumped per beat. When the heart is doing submaximal work, the overall flow of blood is actually *decreased* by training because the now more efficient muscle cells simply extract more oxygen from the bloodstream than they could before training.

Changes brought about by training are less dramatic (but equally important) in the other components of the oxygen delivery system. For all the novice's worry over "wind" and breathing techniques, the lungs appear to undergo only minor adaptations, the primary one being an enhanced ability to exchange carbon dioxide for oxygen in the air sacs (called a lower "alveolar-arterial oxygen gradient"). The vital capacity (amount of expellable air that lungs can hold) can be measurably enlarged when training is initiated during childhood, or when it takes place over a long period of time,[14] although some authorities hold that experiments (probably short term) with adults show no such increases.[15]

As mentioned previously, elite runners do not waste any time worrying about breathing rhythms or techniques. Difficulties in that area are generally reflective of more basic adaptive problems, usually a lack of anaerobic work in training and a consequent distressing oxygen debt in the early part of a race.

Training increases an individual's overall blood supply markedly, and thus increases the total supply of oxygen-carrying hemoglobin (found in the red blood cells). The potential exploitation of this natural adaptation, which is called by the media "blood doping" (but would more appropriately be termed "blood reinfusion"), will be discussed fully in the chapter on racing.

Probably the most important—as far as ultimate racing success—adaptations in the oxygen delivery system occur in the extreme far reaches of its labyrinthine network, in the millions of tiny capillaries which carry the oxygen-laden red cells to the muscles, one at a time. Simply put, distance training seems to promulgate a more diverse and efficient profusion of those tiny tubes, and scientists have found that this leads to a significant increase in blood distribution to muscles when they are engaged in maximal effort.[16]

Because a superior capillary system probably requires more time to develop than any of the other cellular or cardiovascular adaptations, it is probably the reason that the process of developing a world-class distance runner takes a minimum of three to four years.

The fondest dreams of Hollywood screenwriters notwithstanding, a sedentary accountant doesn't quit his job, run a few miles on the beach with a dog, and then make the Olympic team. People who are going to succeed in distance running are like the coal-burning locomotives from days of yore: You can see them coming from a long way off.

Chapter Three

The Training: An Overview

It may come as a surprise to the new runner to find not only that training methods are enveloped in controversy, but that the debate has been one of long standing.

There are, after all, only a few variables in long-distance running: one can run slow or fast, long or short, continuously or with rests. Throw in some geographical considerations (like hills or surf), and perhaps some off-the-wall personal quirks (Zatopek experimented with holding his breath while training), and one has pretty much covered it. There just aren't that many possibilities.

But as we shall see, it is not the number of the ingredients, but the skill of the chef that determines the success of this particular soufflé.

DEFINING TERMS

Preliminarily, we ought to straighten out some terminology. There will undoubtedly be some who disagree with our definitions, and with good reason. Although many of them, which have evolved over a number of years, originated in scientific usage, they have often been popularly distorted to mean something entirely different.

Be that as it may, I use these terms as they are most widely understood by elite distance runners, in the hope of attaining clarity throughout our discussion.

As I define them, there are four basic training techniques, the first two of which are by far the most important.

Overdistance

Long, continuous running, usually away from a track. What is "long" is relative, of course. The term originally meant "longer than racing distance." Thus, if one were a miler, "overdistance" meant any run longer than a mile. What we usually think of as overdistance these days, however, is a run of five miles or more. We see no benefit in trying to use different words to distinguish paces or distances here.

When competitive runners say they're doing "mostly overdistance training," they're not telling you much. The real key, as always, is in the numbers. If they say they're running "120 miles a week at six-minute pace," then you know something.

Intervals

Shorter (between 110 and 1,320 yards, usually), harder runs of a specified distance, with a specified rest between repetitions, usually done on a track or a measured grass field. The great Czech runner Emil Zatopek is generally credited with popularizing the concept; it was associated in its early days with the Hungarian coach Mihaly Igloi, and also with Roger Bannister's occasional adviser, Franz Stampfl, as well as with the Germans Drs. Woldmer Gerschler and Herbert Reindel.

The word "interval" refers to the *rest* portion of the workout, not the running, as some seem to think.[17]

The original idea in true *interval* training was that the actual work would be performed by the heart during the rest (or interval) portion of the workout, as it struggled to repay the quickly incurred oxygen debt. Physiologists had discovered that the heart actually worked harder during these short rest periods than it did during the fast run itself, and they were trying to capitalize on the discovery by getting the maximum work possible from the heart during that phase. Early distinctions were made between "interval training" and "interval work" (which was basically the same thing at a slower pace).

Such distinctions are of little use to us here, and most elite runners have abandoned them. Runners now will occasionally use the term "speed work" to indicate either all-out or almost all-out short fast interval training, such as 100, 220, 330, or even 440 yards, usually with almost total recovery (a rest of sufficient duration to bring the heart rate back to normal).

In writing of interval workouts, it is helpful to understand the shorthand. For instance, 10 × 440 @ 65 w/220j is to be interpreted thus: ten quarter-miles at 65-second pace with a 220-yard jog recovery interval. The type of recovery, whether walking or jogging, is always specified, as it has a great deal to do with the purpose of the workout.[18] There is a world of difference between the intervals described in Phase Three and Phase Four of my own training system, described in Chapter 4, for instance.

Fartlek

The Swedish-developed method, the name of which means literally "play with speed," a romantic notion of unstructured running, generally off the track and through the woods at varying speeds for varying distances, pretty much at the whim of the runner. It is a wonderful concept, full of life and divested of the dreary exactness of the interval field, or the measured road course. It is heartily recommended.

One comment about fartlek, however: Physiologically speaking, it is nothing more than a free-style blend of overdistance and interval training. Very few elite runners these days use much true fartlek in their serious training for the simple reason that, by its nature, fartlek is unmeasured and inexact, relying on the athlete's subjective view of his or her condition and readiness to run hard on any given day. The concept has been partially adapted, however, as a way of spicing up overdistance. Elite runners will often record in their diaries an entry like this: "12 miles overdistance, fartlek second half," which simply means they varied the pace during the last half of the run, threw in surges of 100 or 200 yards, perhaps sprinted up a few hills, and generally gave themselves a tougher workout than usual.

Fartlek training is of particular benefit when an athlete feels overtrained, "stale," or just plain bored. And you may be surprised how often that happens, even in the best of families.

Surge Training

Usually done on the track, it combines continuous pace running with steady surges for specified distances. Sometimes referred to as "pickups," "50-60s" (sprint 50 yards, jog 60 yards), or "straights and curves" (or even, misleadingly, "wind sprints," by Igloi), the technique is designed to prepare the runner for pace changes during a race. Physiologically speaking, the body is being conditioned to call upon the anaerobic system quickly and then to remove the resulting lactic acid after the surge is complete. A typical surge-training session might consist of two miles on the track, with the runner running the straights at race pace and slowing the pace on the curve.

OF GURUS AND MADMEN: A QUICK HISTORY

One point to be made at the outset of any discussion of the evolution of training methods: Distance runners have tended to be the most fiercely independent of almost all athletes. They necessarily spend many hours in introspection, analyzing their reactions to physical stress. They generally tend to think they know more about their bodies than anyone else. Over the years, history has shown they haven't been very wrong about that.

Many successful runners have been self-coached, perhaps with informal advice on training matters from trusted but not dominating quasi-coaches. This was true of Zatopek in the 1950s, of Bannister in 1954 when he ran the first four-minute mile, and of New Zealand's great 3:49 miler, John Walker (though Bannister occasionally consulted with Franz Stampfl and Walker currently talks to Arch Jelly).

It is not that good runners don't want or need coaches; indeed, history has shown that a certain type of coach is actually sought out, even at great distances, by runners in search of the most advanced training wisdom. Such coaches boast dynamic personalities and undeniable qualities of salesmanship (my own college coach, Jumbo Elliot of Villanova, springs instantly to mind).

Such men have, first and foremost, an ability to make athletes believe in themselves and their training. Over the decades several of these men have distinguished themselves by their innovative approaches to training, and by the manner in which they seem to motivate their athletes through sheer charisma.

All too often, however, great runners have found themselves at a point at which they felt they knew more intuitively about their own bodies and training than the coach did from even the most careful observation and the most wide-ranging experience.

Because the most famous running coaches have tended to be "cock o' the walk" types, stern father figures, or unabashed gurus, they have brooked no nonsense. As a result, unpleasant impasses were often reached with their athletes. Ill feelings occasionally became lengthy imbroglios. Peter Snell reached such a point with Arthur Lydiard in the years between his remarkable Olympiads in Rome and Tokyo, but the two were able to patch things up at the last minute, Lydiard worrying all the while that perhaps it was "too late" for him to "salvage" poor Snell's condition. Snell managed quite well, thank you, winning the gold at both 800 and 1,500 meters. But the point is that the reader should approach the pontifications of the great distance coaches with, at the very least, a grain of salt.

Much of running is mental, and the guru-coaches (particularly Cerutty of Australia, Lydiard of New Zealand, and the Americans Jumbo Elliot of Villanova and Bill Bowerman of Oregon) probably have been successful more because they knew how to harness a runner's heart and mind than because of any mysterious secret training formula.

Each of the great coaches has, after all, held some pretty silly ideas over the years (some still do, as we shall see), but the line between stubbornness and tenacity is often blurry indeed. They sensed that much of their athletes' confidence derived from the fact that the coach never lacked an opinion on any matter, no matter how trivial or by what circuitous logic he reached his conclusion. A fictitious example: "Salt tablets? No, a runner should never take pure salt tablets. You never find salt tablets in nature, do you? Therefore, they must be unnatural." That sort of thing.

Over the past several decades first one guru-coach, then another (with an occasional mad doctor-coach or a guru-runner now and again), has reigned as the all-knowing, all-seeing Oz of Aerobic Exercise, each using the club of the undeniable accomplishments of his great athletes (or his *own* accomplishments if he was a self-coached runner) to beat skeptics into submission.

Even Lydiard is not without off-the-wall ideas. For example, he says the following about training in the heat:

> In high temperatures, it's possible to continue steady running for an hour or more, even when the thermometer is near 100°F. But the humidity must also be high, so that the moisture perspired remains on the skin surface to assist with cooling. If the humidity is low and the perspiration evaporates quickly, you'll suffer from dehydration and have difficulty.[19]

The great New Zealand coach claims to have proved his "train in the humidity" theory by personal trial. But it shows a profound misunderstanding of the mechanics of perspiration. Although it is true that there *is* a danger of dehyrdation on hot dry days, a hot humid day presents an equal or greater danger. Perspiration cools the body *only* when it evaporates, taking away the heat with the escaping molecules. [20] The fact that the body is covered with sweat on a hot humid day merely means the pores are producing more perspiration than will readily evaporate, and thus the runner's natural cooling system is overloaded.

It is, in fact, much easier to train in a dry warm climate than a humid warm climate. Of course, precautions against dehydration should be taken. Experience has shown, however, that the runner will more readily recognize the symptoms of dehydration (dizziness, parched mouth, etc.), whereas heat prostration and stroke give much less warning to the inexperienced competitor and thus pose far greater threats to physical well-being.

Lydiard, it should be noted, has demonstrated a self-effacement rarely seen in other great coaches. Unlike many, he is willing to admit that a theory he has held has been shown to be incorrect. He does so grudgingly, however, and because his early theories have been shown to be so uncannily accurate, such exercises in public crow-eating have been rare indeed.

They have been and are great men, the Elliots, the Iglois, the Ceruttys, and the Lydiards. They have contributed much to the sport and are part of its history. They have been colorful, delightful, witty, and life-giving. They have also very often been wrong.

But that is not to take anything away from them. They were often operating on intuition, hunch, and trial and error. The study of exercise physiology is only now beginning to dovetail with the philosophies of the guru-coaches and the innovative self-coached runners. As it does, what is truly amazing about those energetic, dedicated men is not that they were occasionally wrong but that they were so right about so many things without really knowing why.

WORKOUTS: FROM LAZY AFTERNOONS TO LYDIARD

Training theory has changed radically over the years. It was thought forty or fifty years ago that hard running would "tire" an athlete out; workouts were light and the natural aerobic athlete triumphed by sheer luck of the genetic dice.

A miler's afternoon used to include some light jogging, calisthenics, a few wind sprints, and a vigorous rubdown. An athlete might be considered something more (or less) than human if he covered more than two or three miles in a day.

On the other hand, around the turn of the century, before Mr. Ford's tin Lizzie, people walked a great deal more; there was more horseback riding, and more physical labor in general, which probably helps to explain why runners in those early days were able to achieve even the relatively modest accomplishments they did. Thus, a professional runner at the turn of the century named Walter Goodall George ran a 4:12.8 mile, which is still a respectable clocking (albeit more befitting a high school performer these days).[21]

Pre-1900 training theory consisted of a blend of half-truths and superstitions. Much was made of massages, avoidance of the company of ladies, the evils of cigars, and not overtiring oneself. Still and all, George's 4:12 stood as the record for a full 30 years, and it certainly indicates that he and his trainers must have stumbled on a system which entailed good hard work.

THE SCIENTISTS

Before the interval era was ushered in by Emil Zatopek in the early 1950s, distance runners generally trained solely by running longish distances (usually 4 to 12 miles) at relatively slow paces. The reasoning was that if one's race was the 6-mile distance, one should train by running 12 miles half as fast. Besides, in those days, no one really knew what the limits of human endurance were, much less how much time was needed to recuperate after venturing farther and farther into those strange and frightening valleys of fatigue.

The Scandinavians enjoyed preeminence in the 1940s with their fartlek system, and in 1944 the Swede Arne Andersson lowered the mile record to 4:01.6, which surely demonstrated the need for speed as well as endurance training.

But with Zatopek came the curious notion that one could run, on a consistent and organized basis, very hard, very short, and very *many* training runs, and thus accustom oneself to running a long race at a faster pace. Or, as the irrepressible Zatopek then said: "I already know how to run slow. I want to learn how to run fast."[22] The world-renowned Czech was a charismatic figure; running as he did with a rolling head and an agonized expression on his face, he was hard to miss on the track. Off the track he made news as well. Once when he was frisking around with his wife, a javelin thrower, he tossed her into a stream and was dismayed to find out she had broken her ankle. For weeks thereafter, Zatopek insisted on carrying her on his back during his runs through the forest. He did so until his doctor insisted he stop. It was entirely proper that such a man would discover a system of training that would revolutionize distance running and bring about records undreamed of in earlier times. Zatopek won an unprecedented three gold medals in the 1952 Helsinki Olympics.

The interval technique had immediate appeal for the scientifically minded German coaches and theorists; after all, a measured track is much more like a laboratory than the trails or roads. The distances are exact, and the stopwatch tells no lies.

Runners could be put through their paces like so many rats on a wheel; the times were religiously recorded, studied, and filed away for future reference. It fascinated a lot of people, particularly coaches who had long suspected that runners out of observation range on a cross-country course were probably loafing. Interval training kept everyone under the microscope's eye on the track, and no one could ever hide from the cruelty of the unsympathetic stopwatch. And it also was great fun playing around with the formulas on paper: 12 × 330 @ 42 w/110j. That sounds like a fine afternoon's entertainment for the boys.

Then someone developed the more elaborate "stepdowns": 1 × mile @ 4:30 w/440j, 2 × 880 @ 2:10 w/220j, 4 × 440 @ 77 2/110j, and so on. A coach could spend a morning tinkering with such formulas and almost feel as if he had had a workout himself.

It was marvelous! An entire season's workouts could be kept on a few three-by-five cards. Soon after Zatopek retired, everyone was interval-crazy. People were doing intervals in the morning, intervals in the afternoon. Not many observers seemed to notice the figurative corpses strewn along the way, burned out by the mind-ragging routine which strict interval training necessarily becomes. To this day there are thousands of former high school athletes who lived through it all and who still sneer openly when a modern-day jogger goes by. They are casualties of the interval system and they no longer want any part of running. Who can blame them? To them running meant nothing more than endless days of lung-searing 440s and 330s under the scrutiny of a record-keeping tyrant.

But there were some very convincing results brought about by the tough-minded souls who thrived under such pressure. Zatopek, the Briton Gordon Pirie, the Russian Vladimir Kuts, the American miler Jim Beatty, and many, many more used the interval method to make big names for themselves while exploring new dimensions of endurance in the human animal. It appeared that the training riddle was on the verge of being solved once and for all: One had only to juggle the little numbers until the right formula was reached, then just sit back and wait for the gold medals to roll in.

Roger Bannister, a young British medical student, made the biggest breakthrough of them all. His interval-training technique was simplicity itself: Run ten quarter-miles in under 60 seconds with a short (two minute) rest. If one could do that, surely one could put four such quarter-miles together one race day and the first four-minute mile would be accomplished.[22]

In the early spring of 1954, he had finally reduced his average time in the ten-quarter workout from 66 to 59 seconds. Three weeks later, on May 6, 1954, in a well-planned, well-executed assault on an old barrier, Roger Bannister became the first human to run a mile in less than four minutes.

THE AUSSIES

Soon thereafter, a young man in Australia named John Landy began running even faster. His training was said to be as fierce as any yet attempted, with the possible exception of that of Zatopek. Why, Landy was reputed to run as much as 50 miles a week![23]

By sheer force of his ebullient personality, his coach, Percy Cerutty was coaxing the runners at his primitive seaside camp, Portsea, to reach the outer limit of their endurance. No scientific recorder of 440 times was Percy; he believed training should be basically an emotional, joyful, and painful experience. His runners (and Percy too), ran long hard distances, swam in the rugged surf, lifted heavy weights, and drove themselves relentlessly up and down the steep, sandy hill known as "Agony."

Such training within a few years produced an athlete such as the world had never seen before. Both strong and fast, fearless in training as well as racing, he swept all before him. His name was Herb Elliot and he ran times for the mile in the early sixties that would still be respectable today (3:55 and under).[24]

LYDIARD AND THE KIWIS

But soon another set of athletes from "down under," along with their equally captivating coach, were having their say. Marathoner Arthur Lydiard had experimented on his own body for years to find the best approach to physical conditioning. He ran 100 miles a week, he ran 200 miles a week, he ran *more* than 200 miles a week. Slowly his training theories evolved. He used them successfully in his own races, winning national titles in the marathon though he was approaching middle age. Soon he was being sought out for training advice.[25]

With the consistent successes of runners like Murray Halbert in the 5,000 meters and Peter Snell in the 800 and 1,500, as well as several internationally successful marathoners, Lydiard established himself as *the* training theorist of the modern era. Nearly every knowledgeable coach today, whether he acknowledges it or not, uses some form of the Lydiard system.

The original Lydiard system was divided into three distinct phases: marathon training, hill training, and speed training.

The marathon stage was extremely important, serving as the "base" for all future work, the foundation for the elaborate building to be constructed later.

Although Lydiard did not know exactly *why* such a phase was important, he did understand that it was the first step toward superior condition. From a scientific point of view, we now know that his long hard runs (on the border between aerobic and anaerobic pace) were developing the cellular and capillary capacities of his athletes for the arduous tasks ahead. This phase was to last four months. The length of the runs varied during the week, and light jogging generally made the morning workout a recovery time.

The centerpiece of this type of training was the daily long afternoon run, along with the Sunday 20-plus-miler. The goal was to get in 100 hard aerobic miles in addition to some light morning jogging.

The second phase (hill training) Lydiard thought of as merely a bridge between the long, five-to-six-minute-per-mile runs and the much quicker running required on the track. He therefore had his runners "spring" up hills of varying inclines gently descending by a longer route, forming a more or less continuous circuit, the idea being to build the strength of the leg muscles and to develop the racing stride. It is this phase of Lydiard's system which is probably the most controversial and also the most easily dispensed with. Hill training puts a great deal of strain on muscles and tendons, and while it is good hard anaerobic work, it must be done correctly and at the right time of year in order to avoid injuries. Many elite runners ignore the true hill-training phase altogether except to see that they have plenty of inclines on their longer courses. Very few runners who do hill work actually do it as Lydiard suggests, using the slow, springing stride.

The final phase in Lydiard's system was the interval "sharpening" period, during which the runner's racing endurance would be honed to a fine edge. In Lydiard's mind, the whole point of the training cycle was to "bring around" a runner at the right time, which, as observers of the "Olympic letdown" phenomenon know, is not as easy as it sounds.[26]

After a runner completed the interval phase, Lydiard considered him to be fully conditioned and ready to race for the whole competitive season with no further hard work. Lydiard assumed that the races themselves would further sharpen the athlete and thus he counseled that his runners only jog lightly between competitions.

As with others who develop breakthrough methods, the successes of his athletes showed just how well the Lydiard system could prepare an athlete to compete. Within hours of each other, two of his athletes took gold medals in the 1960 Rome Olympics: Snell in the 800 meters, Halberg in the 5,000.[27] Tiny New Zealand, all but unheard of since the days of world-record holder Jack Lovelock of the 1930s, had once again become prominent in distance-running circles.

TODAY

Modern coaches and self-coached runners have tinkered with and refined Lydiard's methods, but the overall philosophy has remained intact.

Ron Clarke, the great Australian distance runner of the middle and late 1960s, quit running altogether when he was a teen-ager, a typical "burnout" from rigid interval training. He got interested again in his twenties because he found marathon training more mentally acceptable.

It wasn't until Arthur Lydiard suggested to him that he needed *both* a base of distance *and* a sharpening interval process, however, that Ron Clarke began smashing world records by incredible margins. Although he had little success in tactical races in the Olympics, Clarke's front-running record performances were so astounding that many experts still regard him as the greatest distance runner ever. For example, on December 18, 1963, Clarke broke the six-year-old six-mile world record by *36 seconds* when he ran 27:17.6 in Melbourne. His 10,000-meter best of 27:39.4 still ranks him as one of the top performers of all time, though he retired in 1969.

Jim Ryun's high school (and later college) coach Bob Timmons, used much of the Lydiard method in developing his great prodigy, the first high school four-minute miler and later the world record holder (at 3:51.3 and 3:51.1).

Lasse Viren's coach, Rolf Haikkola, says that he blends Lydiard's long aerobic runs with Igloi's surge training, Cerutty's hill training, and Paavo Nurmi's steady "pace running" (actually just interval training using longer distances).

Many modern athletes such as Frank Shorter and Bill Rodgers have pretty much disregarded Lydiard's idea of building to racing shape only to slacken off completely during the competitive season. Runners as compulsive as they are probably couldn't handle the inactivity of a pure "racing season," and thus they train year around, as do most runners these days. Obviously they taper off before big races, and they also try to plan out periods of easy running in order to give themselves something of a break.

Shorter's 140-mile-per-week training is uncomplicated: overdistance every morning (seven to ten miles at an easy pace), either a long hard run or else an interval session (of which he runs two per week) in the afternoon, and a 20-miler on Sunday.

The Liquori training system is somewhat different. The intervals are shorter and occasionally faster, and the overall mileage total is probably closer to 100 per week, but the basic approach is very similar.

Many elite runners today make no attempt to break their training up into "base" and "sharpening" (or "aerobic" and "anaerobic") stages. These runners generally view their whole career as a building process.

In summary, the Lydiard system (and its various refinements) represents very simply the state of the art in modern distance-running training.

Perhaps someone will come along with some new breakthrough concept and we'll see another round of world records by his or her athletes, but it doesn't seem likely.

Lydiard, through trial and error, stumbled onto training ideas which mesh well with recently discovered scientific knowledge. There *is* a need for a base of long endurance runs because mitochondrial and capillary development cannot be as efficiently accomplished in any other way; there *is* a way to "sharpen" an athlete by interval training, perfecting the anaerobic pathways and training the muscles to survive and dispose of the lactic acid necessarily generated at racing paces.

It is therefore not surprising that Lydiard's basic theories are still intact long after his original batch of great runners have hung up their famous black racing vests with the silver fern on the breast.

Lasse Viren, who may yet prove himself to be the greatest distance runner of all time, owes no more to his own coach than he does to Lydiard. It was Lydiard, in fact, who was hired by the Finnish government in 1966 to revamp the flagging national training program, and it was the program he helped establish that subsequently produced the great new

Flying Finn.[29] Thus when Lydiard claims credit for most modern running theory, he is not far off the mark.

The training methods of Sebastian Coe, a world record holder in the mile at 3:49:0 flat, are basically those of the New Zealand coach,[30] as are those of the former record holder and fellow New Zealander John Walker, who is, for the most part, self-coached.

The "innovations" in racing during the past decades have been minor in comparison to Lydiard's. Altitude training, carbohydrate loading, blood reinfusion, electrolylte drinks, megavitamins, vegetarianism, bee pollen, and the $75 training shoe all indicate that, as far as basic training concepts go, the great Kiwi coach pretty much led us to the top of the mountain.

YOUR OWN TRAINING—THE APPROACH

A good basic approach to training can be succinctly stated as follows: Develop a base of several months of long aerobic runs, then begin interspersing several interval workouts per week while attempting to maintain the same mileage level. These interval workouts should be of varying distances, from 220s through 880s, should start at gentle paces but culminate with much sharper sessions as the runner approaches a targeted race. The recovery interval will for the most part be the same distance as the effort run, and will generally (but not always) be in the form of jogging.

That's it. That's the only training strategy you need to win a gold medal in the Olympics. There are, as you might have surmised, a few nuances missing that you will need to consider. You'd best do more than consider them, though. Every good distance runner in the world has them etched on his or her frontal lobes, so it would be wise to take them seriously. These are some of the concepts mentioned earlier which sound so simple they are easy to dismiss.

NUGGETS OF WISDOM

Secrets

There aren't any. You might want to tattoo that on the back of your hand. Anyone who says there are shortcuts in this business is probably trying to sell you something. That's it: no secrets. Not herbs and spices, not $75 training shoes, not bee pollen, not carbohydrate loading, not caffeine loading. Any "secrets" there are to be had can be found within the covers of this book, and since a lot of people (Lydiard and others) have been more or less shouting them at the top of their lungs for many years now, no claim of originality is made here.

Listen to Your Body

No one can tell you when you are overtraining or under-working, or getting stale, or coming down with a cold. Even if someone took daily muscle biopsies and blood samples, they still wouldn't necessarily know any more than a good runner does about his or her own condition at the moment. You have to become adept at judging your own growing abilities and limitations. *This is a very serious component of being a successful runner.*[32] Some athletes *thrive* on 140 miles a week. Others who attempt it turn into a handful of dust and are blown away by the first spring breeze. Consider this: There are successful marathon runners in this country who run as little as 80 miles a week (for instance Benji Durden of Atlanta, who has run 2:10 for the 26.2-mile distance).

When deciding what kind of mileage you can handle at any given time, and when deciding how quickly you can build up to even more mileage, you will simply have to be your own best coach. It is not an easy thing to learn. Some very good athletes never learn how to do it well, and consequently their competitive records are very inconsistent, showing great promise one moment, great disappointment the next.

It's a lonely job, becoming your own coach, but someone has to do it. That someone is you.

The Two-Day-Lag Rule

It usually takes at least one day and more often two for effects (injuries or fatigue) of a hard workout or race to hit you. So don't think you're on the road to Valhalla when you feel wonderful the day after your first 65-minute ten-miler in training. Best to wait another day. This is a time when a lot of people overtrain or injure themselves, particularly after a race. It's best to rely on the simple, objective evidence of your training calendar. If you *know* a 65-minute ten-miler is a hard effort for you (perhaps because you've never been able to do one before) then you must automatically assume the next day ought to be rather easy. The day *after* that you'll congratulate yourself for being so foresighted.

The Consistency Ethic

If you have pneumonia, you're going to have to hang it up for a while. If you get an injury that can't be "run through," far better to let yourself heal up than to stick your chin out and proceed to train until you cripple yourself. (Oh, we *are* long suffering when we want to be, aren't we?) But, otherwise, don't miss a workout. Once you miss the first one ("Well, we were due at the party and my wife has been getting pretty burned about this running deal anyway . . ."), it is much easier to miss the second one ("Well, the ball game was coming on the tube and . . .").

The consistency ethic will get you into your shorts and

out running around an airport between planes to get your morning workout in. Why not? Better to be a fanatic about running than about television or French cooking (better yet, be a fanatic about running *and* about television and French cooking).

Goals

You're going to have to set some realistic goals in order to know if you're making progress. It is not enough to say: "I'm going to keep knocking twenty to twenty-five seconds off my ten-thousand-meter time until I get down to world-record level."

The operative word in the first sentence is "realistic." Do not circle the date for the Olympic 10K final yet. Pick yourself a race you know you can get into, give yourself plenty of time for proper training (preferably at least six months), and then set up a realistic training program for running that one race "all out."

You can run other races in the meantime, but you should not take them very seriously. Nearly all elite runners approach their racing in such a manner. The fact that they often win races they aren't pointing for simply means that they are that much better than the available competition. But we all are becoming more and more vulnerable to the good local or regional runner who is pointing for a race against us.

"Running through" a race simply means training right up until the day of the race as if it weren't going to take place. One thus places oneself at a disadvantage for the race by being tired from training, but one's long-range goals are more important than winning everything one enters.

It is not as easy as it sounds. It takes great discipline to intentionally remove your competitive edge the day before you run against that smarty-pants Herb Stanwick from Accounting, who has been trying to put your scalp on his belt for eight months. If he beats you, just smile and tell him you're "training through." Invite him to show up at the starting line of your target race.

You might even surprise yourself and start running pretty well in nontarget races even though you're tired from training.

Training Diary

Keep one. Some people keep their training records on a calendar, some in an actual diary format. No matter. What is important is to be able to look back and learn from your training experience. Often your day-to-day subjective feelings can't give you the big picture the way more objective notations can.

Be sure to record the length of your runs, the time (or, if you don't like the pressure of timing yourself, your best guess as to pace), how you felt, whether you felt a twinge of an injury coming on, weather conditions, and anything else that might become relevant later on. This kind of record is invaluable in assessing your training and its effects on your body.

Review your training records often, and be sure to record the day's effort while it is still fresh in your mind. A well-kept training diary will be of great comfort to you when preparing for the target race. It will help to convince you that you have truly readied yourself for the test.

Moderation

Much of our discussion has centered on all the hard, consistent work you will have to do to become an elite runner. But here is a true "secret" that even a lot of very good runners have difficulty mastering: The biggest challenge facing the ambitious, talented runner these days is not making him- or herself work up to the maximum, but in knowing when he or she is working *beyond* the maximum, and thus hurting the overall effort.

So much more is now known about training methods and physiology that the real challenge is in learning when to push on through old barriers and when to back off (thus avoiding lost time to injuries or illness).

That is why the would-be elite runner *has* to learn to judge his or her own progress, to learn his or her own strengths and weaknesses, to learn how quickly he or she can build up the intensity of training.

Anyone who gets all excited about becoming a champion runner can go out and kill himself or herself for three days in a row. Every freshman cross-country runner who ever arrived on campus in the fall itching to establish a place in the pecking order has done it at least once (some keep doing it every year).

The real test of a runner is to make it through his other projected mileage (whether 50 a week or 100 a week) for three months and still be able to walk on his or her own feet by the time the national championships roll around. You'd be surprised how many good runners fail that test every year.

Friends and Other Strangers

Training with a group of his "mates" was about the best part of his day, Ron Clarke used to say. And it can truly be a fine way to cover mileage and establish very close and long-lasting friendships. But there are some dangers in group training, particularly for the relatively inexperienced runner.

The first thing one should be sure of before hopping in with a group of fellow runners is that they are on more or less the same general fitness/ability plateau as you are.

Getting in with a much more talented or fit group can be physically counterproductive as well as spiritually discouraging. Be honest about it. If you really want to train with a faster set, do it every other day, giving yourself an easier run in between. If you get teased about taking "vacations," your ego can take it. They're just getting the obvious out in the open anyway. Runners are notoriously aware of who is better than whom, and are generally more open about it than other athletes. The results come out in black and white anyway. There is a time and a place to revise their opinions, and that time and place is at your target race.

The word on group training is: It's great if it works. If you are drawn to a group that likes to race each other every day, forget it. You can make better progress on your own. No one has ever become an elite runner by winning a morning training session.

Two-A-Days

So this is how the real fanatics do it, eh? Well, fine. I'll meet you tomorrow at 6 A.M. by the barking dog on the corner.

Hold on just a second. You want to make this process as easy on yourself as possible, right? After all, things are going to get plenty tough later on all by themselves, so why not give yourself a break whenever you can?

There seems to be no real benefit to be gained from dividing up your training into two sessions until your daily mileage gets up to 15 a day or so. Why? Because, contrary to popular opinion, you want to get *away* from running as much as possible when you're putting in between 50 and 100 miles a week.

So why *immerse* yourself in the thing before you're even physically able to do that kind of mileage? In short, it is not only presumptuous but also largely unnecessary to divide a ten-mile day into five in the morning and five in the afternoon. Most experts now agree that you'll get better results from a single ten-miler anyway. If you are a natural early bird and want to get it all done in the morning and then forget running for the rest of the day, have at it.

If and when you do start a second daily session, it will be pretty tough on your system, no matter how "invigorating" you tell yourself hopping out of the sack at 5:30 is the first day. The key is to break in very slowly. Keep up your normal afternoon run and add a two-mile jog in the morning. It will flush out the system and get you moving. Think of it as a pump-priming operation rather than a serious training session. Keep it up for a week without letting your other training suffer. Then look back and evaluate how much more you can handle, if any.

Just remember this: Once you're into a two-a-day training, you're on a different plateau entirely. The Consistency Ethic still applies and woe to him who begins missing his or her "morning." When you're going twice a day, sometimes it feels like you're doing nothing but running, showering, eating, and then running again.

As enthusiastic as you might be at this very moment, an alarm clock with the hands set at 6 A.M. can get to be a *very* annoying sight. And remember: *Many, many* excellent runners never felt it necessary to go twice a day.

Flexibility

Just as it is axiomatic that the easiest way to cover long mileage on a daily basis is to run familiar courses, one must also have the flexibility to train on a catch-as-catch-can basis whenever the imperatives of daily life take you away from your routine.

"I am a master of the 'out and back course' in a strange city," Frank Shorter once said. He then proceeded to get hopelessly lost, running a few extra miles to find his hotel again.

Keep it Familiar

Most elite runners are aware that carrying a heavy mileage load on a daily basis becomes psychologically wearing over a period of time. They look for ways to make it as gentle on their psyches as possible, and one of the best ways to do so lies in the careful selection of their running courses. Some popular "wisdom" has it that you should run a different course every day. That is not true. A runner should have a rather small number of courses of varying lengths, and he or she should stick to them. Once a course becomes familiar, it does not loom in the mind as such a formidable obstacle. The landmarks become familiar, friendly. Changes in terrain (otherwise known as "hills") become predictable and the mind is prepared to tackle them in advance.

But as every rule has its exception, so does this one. Read this section in conjunction with the "Flexibility" section. And keep this example in mind: Occasionally Bill Rodgers, out of sheer boredom with all his courses, perhaps tired of sidewalks and traffic and conversation, will go out for his afternoon run and just bust ten miles on the track all by himself. Forty times around the old quarter-mile oval, hard. Contrary to all the current thinking, probably contrary to his *own* advice, he does it nonetheless.

We runners are more complicated animals than we sometimes think, and we haven't yet completely figured ourselves out.

Shoes

It should be obvious to most experienced runners that entire volumes could be (and have been) written on the subject of running shoes. This short discussion will be solely an effort to get you pointed in the right direction. In order to save time and avoid overly complicating an already confusing area, here are a series of undocumented but widely held beliefs (among elite runners) concerning their footwear.

1. There aren't any secrets. Shoes cannot help you run much faster, no matter how good they are. What they can do is help you to cover your mileage over the hard surface of twentieth-century asphalt America without injuring yourself too badly.

2. Runners are different. Many have feet that turn outward, many others roll inward: two entirely different problems which will probably require entirely different kinds of shoes.

3. Shoe manufacturers haven't shown much interest in dealing directly with the different problems different runners face. Thus we have seen innovations that not only have been unhelpful, but have probably *added* to runners' injury problems. The ultraflared heel is one such example; the highly elevated heel is another.

Because few runners land evenly on their heels, the flared heel caused a twisting shock wave in the area of the achilles-tendon attachment site, which in acute cases was transmitted up as high as the knee. Result: achilles and knee injuries.

When unaccompanied by a highly cushioned ball area, the highly elevated heel creates the same problem as women's high heels create: shortened calves and tight achilles tendons. Thus when the runner comes down off his or her elevated to run in racing flats (or to run barefooted down the beach), Mother Nature steps in and reminds you what you have done to yourself by that nice, unnatural cushy heel strike. Result: achilles problems.

Many runners who have been around awhile are aware of all this simply because they remember the days when the long-distance shoe had not been developed and distance runners trained in shoes that were really not much more than "flats" for sprinters to wear before they put their spikes on. Shoes like the Adidas Gazelle did not provide a great deal of cushion, but they were approximately the same height at the ball as at the heel. The Italia was an even earlier example.

The point? Simply this: It is almost impossible to find anyone among old-time elite runners who can even remember anyone having achilles problems before 1973 or so.

4. Like much of your training program, you are going to have to figure out your shoe situation yourself. You are an

individual, with individual problems. The basic advice is to go for a shoe that approximates nature as closely as possible. You need heel cushioning because asphalt and concrete are not found naturally covering the countryside. But to bring that into balance, you should also look for ball-of-the-foot cushioning as well.

Experiment with several models and when you find one that seems to give you protection for several hundred miles, go out and buy as many pairs as you can afford before the manufacturer decides to "improve" on it for you. This is the best possible advice that you can get on shoe purchasing. Magazine shoe ratings are often misleading, inaccurate, and sometimes occasionally downright dishonest. You can learn more from your fellow runners (particularly those with the same general problems you have) than from reading all the quasi-scientific analyses.

5. Improve on your shoes and make them last. A hot-glue gun works pretty well, so do products like Shoe Goo. They are worth the effort because a pair of broken-in shoes that are working for you is not something you can go out and buy, for any amount of money. If something on your shoe is irritating your feet somehow, and you figure out what it is, *cut it off*. Don't be afraid to modify the product. The important thing is your body and how it holds up to the pounding, not how lovely that little stripe looks on the side of your new Kazoom Night Flyers.

Another helpful idea is to use several pairs of shoes all the time. Rotate them even though you have developed one favorite pair. This will help prevent your favorites from getting too worn all at once and thus start causing injuries. Also, you should keep even your really broken-down shoes for (literally) rainy days. You will find yourself running in slush and sleet from time to time and there is no point doing it in your better shoes. Unless your oldies are *really* decrepit, it is not likely that running for one day in them will cause any serious injury problems, and they can help add several hundred miles to your better shoes by sparing them the harsher elements for a while.

Thus, the word on shoes is much like the word on training: The most important conclusions have to be reached by *you*. Distance running has long been a sport for thinkers; so start thinking.

Orthotics and Mother Nature

This is yet another area where the runner is going to have to figure things out for him- or herself. Many runners have had apparent success using the artificial reinforcement which orthotics represent. Just remember Mother Nature doesn't leap for joy every time man thinks he has again improved on her work. Orthotics are designed to take a foot "problem" and correct it by means of specially designed shoe inserts whose purpose is to simulate the "normal" biomechanics of foot strike.

Many runners have benefited from such devices while many others have graduated to other, more mysterious ailments after using them. Further, many runners have successfully diagnosed their own problems and counteracted them by making their own devices (i.e., heel pads for achilles irritation). Thus we find ourselves once again at the conclusion that no one discipline, not podiatry, not orthopedics, not witch doctoring, has cornered the market on distance-running truths. The best advice, again, is that variation of *caveat emptor:* runner beware. And be *aware*, of your own problems and of the solutions you might try.

Some top road runners do wear orthotics; however, most track runners (who race in spikes) do not. I believe that orthotics are supports for weak ligaments and tendons in the feet and that constant use of orthotics actually causes those ligaments and tendons (as well as the muscles which support the foot) to atrophy somewhat, thus ultimately defeating the whole purpose of wearing them.

It is perhaps not noticeable in training flats, but when a runner who trains with orthotics puts on spikes to race and gets up on his toes, watch out. The foot now is no longer being supported, and the weakened muscles and supporting tissues tend to break down.

I therefore recommend that runners wean themselves off orthotics as soon as they can, after using them to get through a chronic problem or injury. For some runners, however, orthotics are probably the only answer to extreme problems in the foot and knee, and for those runners the benefits of wearing them far outweigh the long-term risks.

BREAKING DOWN

This phrase, often used by elite runners, refers to the physiological (as well as psychological) bankruptcy you will surely learn about if you do not remember the Two-Day-Lag Rule, the Moderation Rule, and the simple wisdom your mother used to try to give you about not "overdoing a good thing."

Breaking down is the result of serious overtraining. It will usually take several days of such overtraining to accomplish, but when it arrives you will know it. You will have little or no energy, not just for running, for *anything*. You will be cranky, restless, unable to sleep or rest well. You will have little in the way of appetite, though your body will be in dire need of glycogen. You will get depressed. You will think about giving up running as being too silly a preoccupation for a civilized human being.

Breaking down usually is a result, strangely enough, of some particularly high point in a runner's career. He or she will have just arrived at a summer running camp and gotten in an average of 15 miles a day for three days, more than ever before. All of a sudden the Olympic trials begin to loom on the horizon. He or she goes out on the fourth day for a ten-miler and it all disappears like a ghost in the night.

The runner has reached the breakdown stage, and it will take several days of nearly complete rest to get out of it. The system has become nearly totally depleted.

The best advice available for this trying period is: (1) Cut both mileage and pace severely. Jog two or three miles just to flush the system out. Anything further that you put into these runs will just prolong your agony. (2) Eat carbohydrates and sweets to replace your depleted glycogen. (3) Get plenty of rest, even afternoon naps. (4) *Relax.* Forget about running for the most part. Read about sailing, mountain climbing, high finance. And remember all the while: Like most of human experience, you aren't the first and you won't be the last to undergo it. Like all things, "breaking down" too will pass.

BREAKING UP

"The more runners run, the more conflicts they experience with spouses or close relatives," said a recent article in *Parade* magazine. The article went on to quote a poll taken in the Boston area which indicated that runners who averaged more than 70 miles a week were "far more likely to have marital problems than occasional or moderate runners."[32]

All of which merely restates a truism that elite runners have lived with for a long time: It's hard to keep a mate happy and train hard at the same time.

The training diary is a jealous mistress indeed, and anyone who undertakes serious competitive training ought to be aware of that Boston poll, which warns ominously: "Nearly half the full-time runners admitted that their partners felt neglected. In 40 percent of the cases, the friction from running was serious enough to lead to divorce."

NUTRITION

Elite runners are often asked what they eat. It drives them crazy. Very few have rigid diets, although many have overall philosophies on nutrition which they try to follow as best they can.

Many go by what might be called the Pregnancy Dietary Law, which simply states that if you feel like eating artichoke hearts, eat artichoke hearts. The theory here is that a body being pushed to its physical limits will generally respond naturally to whatever its deficiencies are; the runner need but listen carefully to the messages. Shorter has long mystified and delighted magazine writers by munching on a Twinkie or some other form of "junk food" during an interview. It is reported in print, of course, and the next day there is a run on Ding Dongs, Banana Flips, and Moon Pies as runners rush to their grocery shelves in a mad scramble to buy out the new "secret." Actually, there is considerable evidence these days that there really isn't any such thing as junk food,[33] and it turns out that Shorter has merely been satisfying his need for carbohydrates, especially sugar, by such dining habits.

The recommendation here is that runners should generally eat pretty much what they feel like, and that generally speaking their diets ought to consist to a great extent of carbohydrates. Fats and proteins are essential as well, though not in as large quantities. Since it is very difficult to balance the body's metabolic equations on a strictly vegetarian diet, vegetarianism for runners is discouraged from this corner. One 1972 Olympic 10,000-meter runner had a fling at strict vegetarianism but found he had to retreat to a "fish and fowl" compromise because the added dietary complications (particularly when traveling) made training simply too much of an ordeal.

Another area of dietary controversy is vitamins. The recommendation in a nutshell is that the runner approaching ten-miles-a-day training probably should take some form of dietary supplement.

Although many nutritional experts disparage the taking of vitamins, claiming that a "balanced diet" provides everything a person needs in the way of nutrition, such an argument begs not one but two questions. The first is: In a society where the most popular food seems to be junk food, just who is eating "balanced" meals these days? The second harkens back to an earlier observation, which is simply that most experimentation on health and nutrition up until recently has concerned itself with "average" folks. Very little work has been done on the dietary needs of extraordinary athletes training near the frontiers of human endurance on a daily basis.

One experiment that *did* concern itself with such a problem indicates that an athlete in serious competitive training may indeed require a nutritional supplement. A study in Moscow on seven men undergoing very strenuous physical and mental cosmonaut-type training demonstrated that daily doses of "nutritional correction supplements" along with a standard diet would in fact enhance physical and mental performance. The supplements included glutamic and aspartic acids, methionine, B vitamins, vitamin C, vitamin A, rutin, nicotinamide, nucleic acids, and organic potassium, calcium, and magnesium salts.

The results: "Physical performance increased . . . working rate increased significantly. Coordination of movements improved in step testing and spatial orientation . . . time for decision making was reduced . . . heart rates during exercise were significantly lower after [supplement] intake. Intake of [the supplement] reduced the level of tremor."

The conclusion of the study, as interpreted by the *Journal of Sports Medicine*, was "Such [supplements] may become a promising tool in optimizing the health and performance of men working in unusually demanding circumstances."[34]

Thus, only a few years ago a runner such as Olympian Jack Bacheler of the original Florida Track Club [who competed in both Mexico City in 1968 (5,000 meters) and in Munich in 1972 (marathon) and who can claim to have greatly influenced the early training of Frank Shorter] was pooh-poohing the idea of practically any kind of dietary supplements. Nowadays, however, we find such eminent physiologists as Dr. David Costill suggesting that nutrition may well be the "new frontier" in distance running performance.[35]

Because the Moscow experiment seems to indicate that dietary supplementation may be of benefit to human beings undergoing stressful exercise, and because there is little or no known danger from the intake of more than "normal" quantities of *most* vitamins (if unused by the body they are merely excreted), the recommendation is that an athlete in serious training might well benefit from *moderate* supplements of vitamins E, A, C, and a B-complex, as well as some form of iron supplement to maximize the oxygen-carrying capacity of the blood.

NUTRITION AND THE RUNNER'S LIFE-STYLE

Food

An ironic situation sometimes develops with many runners who decide to devote their life to training. In the process of running up to 140 miles a week, an individual's life must bend to fit the realities of such a demanding schedule. Many athletes migrate to cities such as Boulder or Gainesville, where there are actually runners' communities, i.e., groups of elite runners who train together.

Such runners often live in a house with six or seven others in order to share both expenses and the common, very unique experience of total dedication to running.

Such rigorous training makes it nearly impossible to hold a job, so such would-be champions begin looking for the cheapest legal way to get food, shelter, and clothing. Eventually they tend to skimp on meals.

Added to this problem is the tendency for runners to skip meals simply because of their tight schedules. It becomes very difficult to eat three meals a day. In my own case, I rarely eat more than two meals a day because it is nearly lunchtime by the time I finish my morning run, then I can't eat for several hours before afternoon training, and some can't eat for two or three hours after a hard run. That doesn't leave much time for meals.

That's why I'm fairly certain that many elite runners run the risk of vitamin and mineral deficiencies. One reported case indicated that a group of highly trained, elite Canadian athletes bordered on malnutrition simply because they weren't taking in enough nutrients to sustain them during the intense training they were doing.[36]

I seem to be able to feel a difference when I am taking vitamins and when I am not. Considering the investment in time I am making to my sport, a few dollars a week for vitamin supplements seems like very little to pay to help ensure that I stay healthy.

Questions about diet are a constant source of amusement to elite runners. When one is running up to 140 miles a week, it is not a matter of carefully selecting the right types of food. We eat everything in sight; everything that we have time to eat. There is little chance of gaining weight when training at such levels. When sharpening or racing, however, it is a different matter.

In my own case, I've noticed that one or two pounds can make a big difference in my performance. My normal weight during the year is around 145 pounds, and I like to train at that weight. For two consecutive years, at the peak of the European season, in one month's time my 5,000-meter time dropped from 13:35 (an average world-class time) to 13:16 (an American record).

It was not a coincidence that this rapid drop in time was

also accompanied by a drop in my body weight from 145 to 141 or 142. In both cases, it was the only time all year that my weight had been that low. I credit the drop to the previous three or four weeks of traveling, being on the road, and not being able to eat my normal helpings of food. The logic of all this is simply that we strive to have a big motor in a small body. If you can have the same amount of strength and endurance at 140 pounds as you did at 150 pounds, then running at 140 will be like running without a ten-pound weight on your back. I have never felt low weight necessarily meant less strength in a race.

Certainly every runner must try to figure out his or her own optimum racing weight, but the average runner simply does not realize how extremely thin the top runners are when they are at their peak condition. In fact, they strike many people as looking a bit unhealthy in their gauntness.

Strong Drink

It is not written on tablets of stone anywhere that runners can't drink and carouse like normal folk on occasion. By now most people know that runners tend to drink their share of the national beer quota. And there are a number of elite runners who do not mind taking a few "pops" of gin and tonic or a bottle of wine with dinner. The key to this puzzle is the Consistency Ethic. A runner in maximum training who is listening to his or her body ought to be able to tell when certain social activities are getting out of hand.

Beer has several beneficial points to recommend it to runners. In the first place it represents fluid replacement, and it does so in a manner that does not throw the body's electrolytes (salts, basically) out of kilter as much as plain water. It also contains a good deal of food value—as anyone with a "beer belly" can tell you—and thus helps keep runners from becoming too thin.

Finally, the mild alcohol content of beer has a relaxing affect on a runner in hard training, and though it might be difficult to imagine, it is possible to be tense after running 20 miles a day for several weeks. The pressure can build up to the point that several elite runners (such as former Olympian Gerry Lindgren) have been known to develop ulcers.

I first found this relaxing effect in 1968 while training at the high-altitude camp at Lake Tahoe for the 1968 Olympic Games. At that time, even though I was a freshman in college, I had never had a beer in my life.

But the combination of altitude and the extremely hard training left me unable to sleep at night. One of my advisers, Pete Peterson, suggested I keep a six-pack of beer under my bed and to have one when I had trouble sleeping. I was soon snoozing like a baby.

Despite the above mentioned advantages to be derived from quaffing a few, there is at least one downside risk that needs to be mentioned. One very elite runner, known for imbibing his share on occasion, on his way to dinner after having just won two national titles in successive nights, confessed a potential personal problem to a friend: He was drinking his normal quantity of beer every day, but he had taken to having a few mixed drinks before dinner, a little wine with dinner, and then more beer later. At the height of his athletic powers, and one of the most highly conditioned athletes in the world, he was sincerely worried about becoming an alcoholic.

Weak Drink

Back in the early days of the Florida Track Club, hot dusty afternoons at the track would sometimes find a fellow in a white lab coat scurrying around the runners. His name was Dr. Cade and he was exhorting exhausted runners to drink a foul-looking purple liquid which tasted more than a little bit like salty dishwater. That was the genesis of Gatorade.

It was also the beginning of a controversy over the efficacy of the fluid, electrolyte, and energy feeding of competitive athletes, a debate which continues in force today.

The topic should be broken down into several components. The first is the race itself. Can an athlete benefit by energy and/or electrolyte feeding prior to or during race? First, the great majority of elite runners avoid any kind of feeding they don't feel is necessary, for the obvious reason that it will slow them down. Thus, on cold days elite marathoners will drink only when they consider it to be helpful, generally during the very early stages of the race.

And for good reason. Several authorities agree that it takes from 15 to 20 minutes before the sugar from special glucose drinks begin to show up in the bloodstream, thus rendering the energizing aspect of the drink all but useless for the shorter races.[37]

Authorities agree that even in the longer races, glucose feedings are a fairly inefficient way of supplying energy to the working muscles, stored glycogen being by far the more important factor.[38] In fact, according to Costill, a prerace feeding of a sugar-rich drink will trigger a release of insulin, which immediately lowers the amount of sugar in the bloodstream.

The real, although limited, benefit to be gained from a glucose drink even during a marathon has a downside trade-off: Race directors, in a misguided belief that more is better, often mix Gatorade, ERG, and other glucose/electrolyte drinks too strongly, and the straining runner may find it difficult to keep down. Many runners find plain water preferable to a sticky sweet glass of some underdiluted wonder drink.

The argument is much the same on the question of electrolyte balancing by use of race feedings. There is no question that the body loses much sodium and potassium while running on a warm day, particularly if the athlete is not acclimated. But there is evidence to indicate that even on successive days of nonintense training in the heat, a normal diet and the body's own adaptations will suffice to keep the electrolytes in balance.[39]

From a practical point of view, however, it is recommended strongly that on especially warm days, runners should make every attempt to drink as much water or weak electrolyte fluid as they can in races of 10,000 meters or more. Barry Brown, a world-class runner at distances from the steeplechase (8:27) through the marathon (2:16), was running comfortably with Bill Rodgers and Frank Shorter in the Montreal trials in 1976 when he was suddenly forced out of the race. He hadn't felt tired at all, but suddenly got into trouble and had to stop. He had difficulty even lifting his legs into the station wagon for the "long ride" back to the finish. What happened?

"I had been training and racing down in the Caribbean and had really gotten heat-acclimated. It was such a pleasure running in that cool, dry Oregon climate that it never crossed my mind what would happen. The other guys were drinking at every station, but I figured, 'what the heck, I'm doing fine' and I never touched a drop. Naturally I was sweating—it was in the seventies—but since it was drying immediately I didn't notice it. I just dehydrated myself out of the race," Brown said later.

It might also be suggested that not enough data have been gathered to know conclusively whether athletes need supplementary electrolytes during the normal course of daily training.

Dr. Costill feels they do, and it is a fact that there is a substantial increase in business at the Red Lion Tavern in Gainesville when those warm spring days roll around and the Florida Track Club finds itself en masse consuming huge quantities of salty popcorn and its own carbonated, sudsy electrolyte fluid (usually by the pitcher).

Nor is scientific evidence lacking to back up that proposition. A recent study at the University of Florida has shown that heat-acclimated runners could maintain a positive potassium balance, even running 18 to 20 miles per day, by taking a 3.8-gram potassium supplement per liter of body fluid; if however, the supplement was cut drastically—to .17 grams per liter or to no supplement at all—the runners went into subclinical potassium deficiency. Research has shown that even a subclinical deficiency of this important body salt can lead to *muscle cell destruction.* Potassium is essential in maintaining muscle relaxation, intracellular acid-base balance, and for osmotic pressure regulation between the cells' walls.

The researchers recommended that runners training in hot climates take in excess of three grams of potassium per day, but because of dangers from too rapid absorption in the intestines, it should be taken not in solid form but rather in the form of high-potassium fruits such as oranges or bananas (five to eight servings per day) or in an electrolyte drink.[40]

In summary, the value of electrolyte/glucose drinks is minimal in races of less than ten miles and/or when temperatures are less than 70 degrees. On warm days it is recommended for safety's sake, if for no other reason, than the athlete get as much prerace and during-race fluid intake, and that ideally this fluid should be a properly mixed electrolyte drink such as ERG or Gatorade or one of their numerous imitators.

It is also recommended that runners who train daily in the warmer climates keep their potassium levels up, and that the best way to do this is through a high intake of potassium-rich fruit and/or electrolyte drinks.

In both racing and training, the value of glucose feeding to provide energy is almost totally without value, particularly when compared to the body's other sources of energy, in particular muscle glycogen and free fatty acids.

Carbohydrate Loading

This technique has received a great deal of attention in the popular periodicals and from the less knowledgeable (but still widely read) writers on the subject. Carbohydrate loading is based upon the sound scientific finding that when the body is intentionally depleted and subsequently deprived of glycogen, it will overstore such fuel when it becomes available again.

Thus the correct way to build up a surplus of muscle glycogen is to run to depletion (which may mean a 20-mile run for an elite runner) about six days before a big race. The runner then does no training nor does he eat carbohydrates for several days. About three days before competition, he overloads his system with carbohydrates, which his deprived body stores greedily. Through this technique much more glycogen can be shoehorned into the cell's energy reservoir, which is no small consideration in a marathon or ultramarathon situation.

The problem with the traditional carbohydrate loading process is that it shocks the body and the psyche at a time when the runner needs all the calm and rest he or she can get. In addition, most elite runners find they do not like to cut back their training to the extent required by the technique. They simply go stir crazy when deprived of "enough" exercise. The recommendation here is in accord with respected authority in the field: Sufficient carbohydrate loading can be accomplished by simply lightening the training load five to seven days before an important competition, and by ingesting more carbohydrates than usual.[41]

Such a recommendation seems to conform to the Pregnancy Dietary Law as well. Elite runners seem naturally to begin craving carbohydrates when they ease up on their training. We do not know *why* this happens (indeed, it may very well be psychological: the anticipation of the race and the runner's knowledge of nutrition).

Such "carbing up without tears" avoids the trauma of the depletion run, as well as the shock of carbohydrate deprivation for the several days afterwards, and allows the runner to train with adequate intensity to keep from bouncing off the walls from the excess energy he or she would have with little training. This method of increasing muscle glycogen doesn't have the romance and glamour associated with the formal carbohydrate loading process, but it has become the most widely accepted method among elite runners.

Caffeine Loading

Recent research indicates that ingestion of caffeine before strenuous running will stimulate the release of free fatty acids, which are an important fuel source in the longer distances.[42]

Caffeine has been used as a training stimulant (for runners as well as weight men and other athletes) in East and West Germany, as well as other countries with sophisticated training programs.

There is no evidence that using caffeine either in racing or in training is harmful to the body, but the caveat must be offered once again that science often lags behind training trends by several years, and thus we should not expect any timely warnings to come from that quarter. It should be remembered, however, that the runner undergoing the most intense training is very much like an engine operating at its maximum RPMs. The tolerances are critical. Tinkering with the engine may make it run slightly faster for a period of time, but if done without complete knowledge of all the engineering implications, such efforts may bring about dangerous consequences.

However, once again from a practical point of view, many elite runners (as well as athletes in other specialties such as shotput and discus men) are now using caffeine in training. I use it occasionally in training and, from my subjective viewpoint, it does seem to make long runs go easier. Runners particularly interested should read Costill's work in this area.[43]

Stretching

. . . is overrated. Period. Elite runners do stress the necessity of a proper warm-up, however, but that generally entails very little stretching except in the case of special attention to an injury area. With the highly built-up heels of many running shoes these days, it is a good idea to spend a minute or so on some form of achilles/calf stretching, and some other general limbering up, if for no other reason than it feels good.

Generally speaking, however, when good runners speak of a warm-up, they mean starting their run very slowly. The first half-mile might take five minutes or more, the first mile might be as slow as nine or ten minutes. Keep in mind that these are marathoners who can run 4:10 or better for a flat-out mile! If *they* feel it necessary to run that slowly at the beginning of training, it would be wise for those who are not yet so fleet of foot to follow suit.

The word on warming up is: Run at least the first mile, perhaps the first two, *very* slowly. Then stop and do a little stretching after the blood is already pumping. Do as little as three minutes and then go on.

There is entirely too much lip service paid to stretching these days. Elite runners have been bewildered all along by the general stretching hoopla. Because they simply don't have the time, very few of them do even a fraction of what is generally recommended by the "joggers with typewriters" who hand out such tripe for public consumption.

Heat

Hard running in warm weather is the one stress situation that can actually *kill* a highly trained runner.[44] Several world-class runners have come close to death because of their unfamiliarity with heat and their competitive drive taking them too far into territory where the normal safety mechanisms of the body do not function.

That is not to say the body cannot acclimate itself somewhat to heat, or that all runners react the same to heat stress. Many are quite comfortable at temperatures which severely strain others. It has nothing to do with nationality. A Scandinavian runner may find that he adapts well to racing in southern climes; an African may have difficulty. But the body's adaptation to heat stress is *not* the same sort of thing as the body's adaptation to high altitude. What happens in heat adaptation is that the system learns to retain electrolytes rather than sweat them out, thus preventing premature imbalance in that system and accompanying distress.[45] In altitude training, the body's adaptation to the lesser amounts of oxygen in the air actually makes the runner *stronger*, giving his bloodstream a more efficient oxygen-carrying capacity. It has been theorized that a similar effect takes place when a runner trains in the heat, and then competes in a cooler climate. However, the experience of runners like Jack Bacheler, who trained for a long time in Florida's protracted hot summers, seems to indicate that a moderate or cool climate is more conducive to higher workloads than is a very warm climate. Training in a moderate climate also makes the body more adaptive to heat stress situations. Bacheler reports: "I remember one summer it was very hot as I was getting ready for the AAU five thousand and ten thousand to be held in Miami. I had been actually increasing my mileage up to around twenty-three or twenty-four miles a day—I even added a third workout at noon, just to be really prepared for the heat—but my competitive times indicated that I was very slowly losing my conditioning even though I was actually training harder."

I think that training in moderate heat can be of the same kind of benefit as altitude training to runners who travel to a cooler climate to compete. Training at altitude increases the hemoglobin content of the blood. Training at sea level in the heat increases the total volume of the blood. The ultimate advantage, therefore, would accrue to an athlete who trained at altitude in a warm climate. For this reason, some European runners, among them Lasse Viren, go to Brazil and other parts of South America to train at altitude rather than cooler altitude sites such as Switzerland or Colorado.

I believe the increased blood volume caused by heat training can be beneficial to the athlete, but there is always a point of diminishing returns. The heat is so great in Florida at times that it clearly affects the runners' ability to complete their scheduled workouts.

Heat also presents serious psychological problems. It is difficult to believe that you are going to be able to run a four-minute mile in Europe in a week when you are having trouble running ten miles in 61 minutes.

In 1977 I was the American representative in the 5,000 meters at the World Cup meet. I had trained hard in Florida through a desperately hot July and an equally hot first two weeks of August. The average daily temperature had been around 95 degrees, with very high humidity.

Two weeks before the meet I was wondering if I should waste my time traveling to Europe for the race. My workouts were so slow I felt it would be embarrassing even to try to compete at the world-class level. I was totally drained, both physically and emotionally, by the weeks of intense heat training.

Barry Brown, my long-time training partner in Gainesville, assured me that it was only the heat. I flew to Nice for a 1,500 "tune-up" race. Although I had not run a competitive race for six weeks, I found myself with the leaders with one lap to go. Mike Boit and Wilson Waigwa were on my tail, and I knew from experience they both had fierce kicks. With 300 yards to go, I said to myself: "I can't win this race, but I feel good, so I'm going to blow it out." When I let go, no one else came with me.

That was an eerie feeling, going down the backstretch of a

stadium with no stands on that side, hearing nothing but the sound of my own foot-strikes in a world-class race.

I won in a time of 3:38, the equivalent of a 3:55 mile. Two nights later, I ran the 5,000 meters in Zurich against the best field to have been assembled in four years, including the Olympic final in Montreal (which didn't contain the Africans).

None of the other runners had heard about my performance in Nice two nights earlier; thus I was a very dark horse among the likes of New Zealander Dick Quax (the world record holder), Ethiopian Mirus Yifter, and Kenyan Henry Rono (among others).

Again, I struck with one lap to go and it was quickly over. I won the race by two seconds in an American record time of 13:16.1. I must admit that I was as surprised as anyone in the race. Ten days later, at the World Cup meet, I lost to Yifter by two seconds, again breaking the American record with a time of 13:15, which still stands today (1980).

And only a few weeks earlier I had been wondering whether I should even make the trip!

It is sad to have to report to runners in the hot, humid South, but you will never post good times when it gets warm below the Mason-Dixon Line. My subjective judgment is that it will be almost impossible to set world records at distances of 5,000 and 10,000 meters (or longer) in temperatures in excess of 55 degrees.

But training is a different matter. I think running in 85 or 90 degrees in Florida, Tanzania, or Kenya can be a boon to training, so long as the temperature and humidity don't get so high as actually to limit the amount of work the athlete is able to put in every day.

Altitude Training

Here is another area that has probably received too much in the way of media attention. The scientific principle behind training at altitude is sound : The body responds to the lessened oxygen content of the air by enriching itself with more hemoglobin. The altitude-acclimated runner then descends to sea level and runs away with races against mere mortals.[46] It makes for a nice romantic fable. But even such an altitude advocate as Frank Shorter will readily admit these days that the prime attraction of Boulder, Colorado, is not the altitude but the simple fact that he likes living there. "You train best in places where you like to live," he says.

What the nonelite runner does not seem (or want) to recognize about most of these "secrets" is that they will improve his finish in a race by but a few steps, and in order for those few steps to become crucial the runner must of necessity be operating at the outer edge of his or her capabilities, where even the longer races are decided not by seconds but fractions thereof. One has but to look to Jeff Wells's incredible and almost successful sprint against Bill Rodgers in the Boston Marathon in 1978 to see how fine a line may divide gold from silver when great runners meet. In that case the difference ended up being two seconds (2:10.13 to 2:10.15) after 26.2 miles!

The Hard/Easy Ethic

This goes hand in hand with the Consistency Ethic, as well as the Two-Day-Lag Rule, although some might think they see a contradiction. The idea is simply that one cannot train at 110 percent effort daily and not expect to end up flat on his or her back after about five days. The body requires both the stress of exercise *and* the serenity of light days (please note, however, that a 15-mile day is considered "easy" by many elite runners) in order to grow stronger and faster.

Thus when you read something in this book which seems to indicate that a runner must train as hard as he or she possibly can every day, that is not what is meant.

"Maximum training" is what is meant, and maximum training is simply the hardest training the body can *successfully* tolerate while ascending the various levels of conditioning. That might mean 20 hard miles one day, but only 12 miles of light running the next day.

Believe it or not, even some elite runners never learn the value of light days, never learn to taper off properly before races, and thus never learn the secret of peaking at the proper time for the superhuman effort of an all-out performance. Though some of these performers are extremely talented and courageous competitors (sub-30-minute 10,000 men, sub-2:20 marathoners), they will never reach the peak of the endurance mountain until they master these concepts.

Sex

A topic that has titillated late-night talk-show audiences for years. The interview of a well-known athlete generally goes like this:

HOST: Well, uh, Big Jim, you certainly were firing 'em across the mound when the Stogies won the last game of the series. Tell me something, do you let your wife give you a little action the night before a big game like that, or what?

BIG JIM: Shucks no, Johnny, I tried it but we found out it took seventeen mph off my slider so I gave it up altogether. Wife says she's used to it by now.

HOST: And I bet you've got the happiest milkman in seven counties.

BIG JIM: How'd you know that?

Like much of sports mythology, the "no-sex-before-competition" theory could be written off as total hogwash except for one thing: the very real psychology of aggressive behavior. Just as there are many runners, both male and female, who can retain their competitive edge after bouts with the beast with two backs, there are others who use their libidinous drive to win athletic contests.

Hemingway said he abstained from sex while writing because "the same motor drives them both." There may be something to that; it has long been a cherished tradition in the combative sports such as boxing and wrestling. But abstention during long months of training probably accomplishes little.

The recommendation is simple: If you worry that sex will take away from your athletic performance, it probably will in some way. Put your libido on hold and wait until after the race.

Finally, this true anecdote is offered for whatever value it may have:

Once during the racing season in Europe, two world-class American distance runners (male and female, if you please) spent the entire night before a big meet getting to "know" each other in the biblical sense. Many times, it was said.

The next day she went out and set a world record and he (a sub-3:55 miler) went out and ran a race worthy of a junior high school drum major.

Courage

It's not something that is talked about much by runners, but there is no getting around it: Some of us face the pain or discomfort of the training run or the race better than others. But take heart if you find your courage flagging towards the end of a hard race.

A great deal of pain is actually a fear of the unknown.[47] The elite runner feels the same sensations as all other competitors, but he or she has learned to interpret them not as alarming signals that the body is self-destructing (he or she knows better from long experience), but as indications that the pace may be too fast, warning signs that lactic acid is too high, or that fuel reserves are low.

What is "pain" or "discomfort" to the relatively inexperienced runner is merely information to the elite runner. Physically it feels exactly the same; the difference comes when the brain (conditioned by long hours of training) interprets those tiny electrical impulses.

Blood Reinfusion

A good many elite runners who compete on an international level are now convinced that the Communist bloc countries as well as some Scandinavian countries are experimenting with blood reinfusion. Further, some believe that such pragmatic tinkering around with Mother Nature goes beyond training techniques and begins to invade the province of the Almighty to the extent that neither the Olympics nor the sport of distance running can survive it. One American Olympic champion is reported to have said: "I'm glad I got my gold medal before the dopers got into the sport."

"The dopers" refers to the popular term for reinfusion, which is "blood doping," a process whereby a quantity of an athlete's blood is extracted and frozen while he or she is training. Later, right before competition, the essential elements of the blood (particularly the hemoglobin) are reinjected and the athlete thus enjoys several days of an abnormally efficient bloodstream. Or so goes the theory, anyway.[48]

However, Dr. David Costill and most American experts are unpersuaded by the available literature that blood doping is more of a help than a hindrance in enhancing endurance performance.[49]

The only thing that is certain is that not enough long-term and rigorously scientific research has been done for elite runners to draw final conclusions. One group of scientists reached the same conclusion as Dr. Costill, but by means of an experiment positively loaded down with red flags.[50]

Although in this particular study it was claimed the method

used constituted a "study" on the "effects of blood infusion on endurance capacity with the confounding variables eliminated to a major degree . . . ," one quickly finds more "confounding variables" than anything else.

For instance, one method these particular scientists used to determine the fatigue of the runners on a treadmill was something called a "Rating of Perceived Exertion," which is nothign more than the subject on the treadmill telling someone in a lab coat that he or she is getting pretty tired all right. The fact that such subjectivity is allowed in these scientific inquiries should serve as a caution to elite runners not to blindly accept the conclusions they draw.

Further, the study was performed on "sixteen male subjects" who were "experienced distance runners," no fewer than "thirteen of whom were marathon runners," all of which might be impressive until one considers what constitutes an "experienced distance runner." Or to whom we should extend the title "marathon runner." Is someone who takes a week to run a 26-mile course a marathoner? Not by any useful application of the word. Then we begin to home in on the problem: Is a four-hour competitor a marathoner? How about someone who must walk part of the way?

The reader should understand that this is not an expedition devoted to the gleeful picking of nits. It is an attempt to show how clear thinking on distance-running issues is often derailed by the very people who should be helping to clear up the mysteries.

It is of no surprise whatsoever that the experiment under discussion arrived at this grandiose conclusion: "No significant differences in time to exhaustion or Ratings of Perceived Exertion were observed, although the experimental subjects had significantly higher hemoglobin concentrations than did controls."

So now it becomes apparent just how loosely this experiment (which, remember, claimed to have done away with many of the "confounding variables") was put together.

The two indexes of fatigue—the Rating of Perceived Exertion and the time it took to run the subjects to "exhaustion" on a treadmill—are both entirely subjective.

Anyone who claims that "exhaustion" is a term with any scientific utility ought to return to school for some remedial vocabulary work.

Every elite runner knows that the "exhaustion" one feels after a 29:30 10,000-meter race is every bit as total and compelling as a 28:49, yet the difference in the outcome of the race may be the difference between the olive wreath and the Bronx cheer.

What constitutes "exhaustion" on a treadmill? Could the runner have taken one more step? No? How do we know he is not dogging it, maybe just a little?

The point is that one might get relatively definitive feedback from truly elite runners, whereas with "experienced" runners all subjective data become suspect. Even good collegiate performers could not be expected to give accurate information. How does one arrive at that conclusion? Simple. It has been proved in the laboratory.

In a highly regarded *Sports Illustrated* article in 1973, Olympic marathoner and writer Kenny Moore reported on the first major physiological and psychological testing performed on elite distance runners (the group included Frank Shorter, the late Steve Prefontaine, and Moore himself, a 2:10 marathoner).[51]

Reports Moore: "[One] finding was that at 12 mph on the treadmill a control group of good college runners did not read their bodies well. They said they felt less stress than their oxygen consumption and heart rate indicated—until right before they collapsed. By contrast, world-class runners described levels of fatigue that accurately paralleled their physical states."

Thus it was demonstrated clearly as early as 1973 that subjective feelings of fatigue on a treadmill can only be truly trusted when reported by the highest-echelon runner.

What is the explanation? Moore theorizes, probably correctly:

> An explanation for all this, which appeals to runners, is that the imperatives of racing well call for a certain degree of attention to pace, form, tactics, level of fatigue and liquid intake. Anything, including self-deception, that distracts a runner from the task at hand will be a detriment to performance. In its nuances the pain may be saying something that can help win the race. Rather than distract themselves, the best runners learn to listen.

Precisely.

So, what of blood reinfusion?

Americans must try to understand that most champion runners outside our country are "professional athletes" by American definitions. Many live in what must seem enviable luxury to their countrymen. It is not hyperbole to suggest that these professionals would be willing to take great risks to retain their economic and social status.

And there is this informal yet chilling report from Dr. Gabe Mirkin, which gives insight as to just how rabid for success even American distance runners can become:

> A few years ago I polled more than a hundred top runners and posed this question: "If I could give you a pill that would make you an Olympic champion—and also kill you in a year—would you take it?"
>
> To my amazement, more than half of the athletes responding stated that they would take my magic pill. It is this attitude that explains why drug-taking is such a monumental problem in sports today.[52]

Why would a technique that could perhaps increase the oxygen-carrying capacity of the blood a few percentage points be of that great a significance in a race?

The answer is the same one world-class tennis players give for their extreme dismay over a single line call in a close match. It is simply that such tiny differences can mean the difference between winning and losing, between gold and silver, between lasting fame and haunting obscurity. One has but to recall that the last Olympic 5,000-meter final was won by four-tenths of a second, and that the difference between first and seventh place was less than three seconds!

Could the difference between success and failure in such high-level competition be accounted for by such ghoulish stunts as serving up an extra helping of the athlete's own blood before his event?

The answer, according to some scientists, is yes.[53] Other researchers, such as Costill, say that reinfusion may bring about more problems than benefits (particularly because the added red blood cells tend to increase blood viscosity, thus making circulation more difficult), and that more research is needed before any conclusions can be accurately drawn.[54]

One thing we do know: Several countries requested hospitals in Montreal in 1976 to furnish facilities for the storage of whole blood.

And we also know that many world-class runners are not inclined to believe the doctors and scientists who claim blood reinfusion cannot help performance. We compare it to the anabolic steroids (male hormones) which weight men now consider an *essential* part of their training regimen. Even as we enter the 1980s there are doctors who contend that steroid use doesn't help in power events; some produce studies to back up their contentions.

Not one athlete who has actually taken steroids, however, would agree. The same argument goes for the scientists who claim altitude training is of little or no benefit.

Little wonder that athletes are generally distrustful of the majority of doctors and scientists, choosing instead to believe what they learn from their colleagues and from what their own finely tuned bodies tell them.

One group of athletes who remain totally convinced of the use of blood reinfusion are the New Zealanders. For years now the Kiwis have witnessed at first hand much of the training of foreign runners who go to New Zealand to avoid the European winter. The Kiwis cite retired Scandinavian athletes who have admitted experimenting with reinfusion.

Former mile world record holder John Walker walked up to me after Finn Matti Vainio had pulled a startling upset to win the European championships.

With great consternation he said he could believe it if the guy was bordering on world class and suddenly improved to win a major championship. But he'd watched him train in New Zealand for six weeks, and he clearly couldn't be a runner.

It would appear that the men in the white lab coats now peer out at us from behind every test tube and Bunsen burner.

If they can invade the mysteries of the atom to bring forth the specter of the mushroom cloud, it is not surprising that they can invade the tiled walls of the locker room. It does not stretch credulity too much to claim they have stumbled upon secrets which can be used to steal away the once sacrosanct olive wreath, which the Greeks used to symbolize a prize that had no monetary value, but nevertheless was priceless.

Let us hope that those who say such procedures are useless are, in fact, right. If not, the future of athletics will belong to those myopic souls who tinker among their test tubes and cotton swabs, and not to the strong young men and women who strive and sweat in the spring sunshine to perfect their difficult art, just as their spiritual ancestors did two thousand years ago in the age of Pericles.

Chapter Four

The Training: The Liquori System

THE TWO TRAINING PHILOSOPHIES

There are two separate and distinct approaches to training for foot racing and each has powerful adherents with good arguments to support their position. One school of thought has it that the runner should prepare himself for the One Big Race (such as the Olympic final) and all other races are considered expendable in terms of winning or losing. As a matter of fact, to the One Big Race people, all other races are considered part of training for the big one.

The other approach is simply to build up to a very high level of day-to-day, week-to-week training, and try to win as many as possible, occasionally going for a special peak in order to win the One Big Race. Americans such as myself, Frank Shorter, Bill Rodgers, and others tend to fall in the second category, whereas Europeans, most notably Lasse Viren, fall into the first.

The important thing to remember about the two different

approaches to training is that the Liquori system can be adapted to either philosophy of racing. The fellow who wants to be competitive at a high level every week need only leave off the fourth phase of the system, and he will find himself training *and* racing at close to his personal zenith.

The argument the One Big Race people put forward is a good one. They say that from a psychological as well as a physical standpoint, the body and mind cannot continue to operate on a high plane over the course of several years and still be expected to gather themselves up for the one supreme effort. Better, they say, to plan ahead, train on a low-key basis, and when the time is right put it all together in one sustained drive to the ultimate peak, forgetting wins and losses along the way.

My own personal training philosophy is a combination of the two. Recognizing that there is a good argument for the One Big Race theory, particularly when it comes to the matter of avoiding injuries caused by serious, sustained long-term training, I generally adhere to a compromise between the two philosophies.

When getting ready for a big race such as a World Cup or Olympic 5,000 meters, I lay down a very substantial base of overdistance, slowly programming in more and more intervals, then begin racing at a fairly competitive level, and finally try to achieve the peak by three weeks of very fast speed interval workouts with little rest between repetitions.

In such training, it is often necesary to "run through" races of little consequence, which simply means that no extra time is taken to rest for such races because they aren't worth the loss of training time. That generally means that I will lose some races I ordinarily wouldn't have lost if I had taken the time to go all out for them.

This is a concept well known to the elite runners of today. There was a time when a Liquori or a Shorter or a Rodgers could run through most of their races and still dominate the closest competition, simply because they were that much stronger than the field. Those days are over. "Running through" races is responsible for those strange upsets we often read about in the race results sections of running magazines. "Liquori lost to some guy in Idaho I never heard of!" is the kind of remark generally elicited.

What it means simply is that the regional-class elite runners are rapidly catching up to the top of the field, and if they want to take the time to peak for a local race in order to take a crack at one of the big boys, then they stand a fair chance of putting an impressive pelt on their wall. But before such regional runners go dusting off the shelf in preparation for that Olympic gold medallion, they should understand that while they may have beaten a great runner, they have beaten him at a low point. Most of the big-name elite runners are under a great deal of pressure to race constantly, if for no other reason than it is financially rewarding. They can justify such constant racing only if they make the races part of their training and lose very little mileage in the process. Some have been successful at this process over the years, but the increasing quality of the competition is beginning to tell.

But regardless of which approach to racing you wish to take, the system of training described in this chapter will work for you.

Runners who wish to avoid the ultimate peaking process in order to continue training and racing at a very high (but nonpeaking) level need only omit Phase Four of the system and continue to train and race at Phase Three. Barring stress injuries or illness, a runner should be able to maintain fitness at that level almost indefinitely.

Runners who choose to go through the last three-week peaking phase, though they can expect an ultimate performance from the given training, will have to begin the process all over again at Phase One after the racing peak has been exhausted. The axiom "What goes up, must come down" is apt indeed when applied to runners attempting to get the maximum performance possible from their bodies.

The Liquori system entails a six-month program broken into four distinct phases. I personally feel more comfortable with a program based upon a year's training, but it would be asking a lot of readers to dedicate a year of their running lives to a program that they are not sure will work for them. Thus, I have condensed my regimen into six months, which ought to be adequate for most runners to attain a high level of racing fitness.

It is a totally subjective judgment as to which kind of runner is the greater athlete, the one who has two victories a year and no losses, or the one who races fourteen times and wins twelve. In Finland, the former is considered the ultimate athlete, but I believe in America we respect the athlete more who goes out to face many challenges.

I personally have used both approaches. In high school and college I competed almost every weekend. Because of the sheer genius of Jumbo Elliot, my coach at Villanova, I was able to stay at a peak almost eight months of the year, running a 3:55 mile in January, and continuing to hold that peak until I ran a 3:55 mile in August.

On the other hand, I have used the Lydiard peaking method after college and it enabled me to rise to first and second rankings in the world in 1977 and 1978. It was the Lydiard method that enabled me to go from 13:40 for 5,000 meters in May to 13:15 in July.

For the top-notch athlete testing himself in Olympic competition or against the best in Europe in July and August, peaking *à la* Lydiard is the most desirable approach. Further, if an athlete is close to a world record, peaking is probably the only way to get those extra two-tenths of a second faster than anyone has ever run.

Such an approach has its drawbacks, however. It is difficult indeed to train hard in September for a first race in April. Psychologically, most of us cannot put off gratification for six months to two years without some encouraging signs that we are doing the right thing. Certainly for the athlete who is crushed by defeat, who worries unduly about what his peers think of his performance, the Lydiard method of training will present perhaps insurmountable emotional obstacles.

But whether the runner is going for the One Big Race or for a series of weekend victories, my recommendation is that he or she pick one big race to be the ultimate test for the season, whether that be the Boston Marathon or the runner's college championship. Training should then point toward that long-range objective.

If the runner then chooses to make concessions to the Consistency Ethic in order to pick up some lesser trophies along the way, then that is a matter of simple personal philosophy, and the runner bears the responsibility for any disappointments that may accrue farther down the road.

PHASE ONE: BUILDING THE BASE

This phase, which lasts longer than any of the other three, consists of long, relatively slow runs, once a day, every day of the week except Saturday or Sunday, when the runner will be expected to go out on one very long run, at least 25 percent longer than the longest run during the week. For specifics on this phase, as well as the other three phases, it will be necessary for the runner to refer to the reference charts on pages 116–18 to decide which category of competitor he or she falls into, and thus what type of training he or she will be able to handle in the beginning. For example, an elite runner might well be doing 120 to 140 miles per week during this base building phase, whereas a Class C runner would need only 40 to 60 miles per week.

Purpose

Phase One is designed to get the body ready at the cellular level to perform the heavy demands that will be placed on it later on in other phases and in the race itself. From a physiological standpoint, running long, relatively slow paces will do the following: (1) begin working the heart at 120 to 140 beats per minute, a submaximal effort, but still a stressful, aerobic level of exercise; (2) begin building the cellular mitochondria; (3) begin building the mesh of capillaries throughout the muscle cells which will deliver oxygen and fuel and take away the waste products of exercise; and (4) begin the toning process of the muscles themselves, slowly getting them ready for the more strenuous work ahead.

Length of Phase One

This training period will last 12 weeks (unless you put yourself on the year-long program, in which case you simply double the length to 24 weeks). It is the longest of all the phases simply because the work accomplished during this time is probably the most important of all. It is entirely possible to train by running only very long, relatively slow runs and to achieve moderate success in competition, as several runners of past decades have demonstrated. All successful athletes of the modern era, however, do a great deal more than Phase One type training.

What Phase One Does For You

While you are not yet ready to race at peak levels at the end of 12 weeks of overdistance runs, your body will be ready to move on to more advanced training. You will be more efficient in the mechanical motion of your stride, you will be psychologically stronger because you have successfully been able to handle many miles of training; for many runners there will be confidence-building weight loss, and the built-up tension of forcing yourself to run only at moderate paces will provide some very real momentum when you begin the faster training in Phase Two.

Injury Strategy

As always, the runner should avoid injuries by taking the proper precautions. But since this period is a matter of relatively nonstressful running, there really isn't any excuse for the runner to begin picking up even minor nagging injuries which may plague him later on. It is suggested that the runner run on flat surfaces, avoid hills and other types of rugged terrain which might take away from his goal of maintaining an even, submaximal heart rate, and that the heavier padded shoes be used to avoid foot-strike-type injuries to the foot and knee. This is a good time to use a lot of stretching, and every run should start off with one to two miles of *very* gentle running, which actually is the most important part of warming up. For example, if the afternoon run is scheduled to be ten miles at an eight-minute pace, the runner in Phase One should do the first mile or two at a nine-minute pace or slower.

Even the most elite runners in the world begin their training runs with very slow running in order to avoid injuries caused by simple stiffness prior to exercise.

How to Go About It

Phase One training is the easiest of all training to map out for yourself. For specific guidance on distances, see the reference charts beginning on page 119.

But by way of example, a Category C runner with very little background in training might decide to go for a 50-mile training week. Keeping in mind that he or she will be doing one longer run on the weekend (say, ten miles), that leaves 40 miles to do in six days, or a little under seven miles per day. Knowing the average daily distance, the runner simply juggles the numbers (within reason) to match his or her subjective feelings of fatigue. For example, if your eight-mile run on Monday, coupled with another eight-miler on

Tuesday, has you dragging by Wednesday, there would be no harm at all in cutting back to a five-mile day, or even less. The important thing is keeping the overall quality of your training at a level you can live with (remember the Consistency Ethic?), without having to take unscheduled days off "because I just couldn't run a step!"

By the same token, an elite Category A runner might well be shooting for 100 miles a week during this phase, using a 20-mile run on Sunday as his cornerstone. He would then have 80 miles to divide among the six other days, i.e., about a 13-mile average. That's a lot to bite off in one session a day, and it is not recommended for any but the most experienced and best prepared athletes to undertake.

The reason that the runner is expected to run once a day during this phase, whereas later on he or she may break the training up into two sessions, morning and evening, is simply the goal of this type of training: to elevate the heart level to 120 to 140 beats and keep it there for a certain amount of time.

As a matter of fact, it is almost irrelevant to speak about mileage during this phase because the important factor is not mileage, but *time spent running*. Mileage language is used simply to keep the discussion consistent. But the runner should keep in mind during this early phase that it hardly makes any difference how far or how fast he or she is running, just so long as 40 minutes or more elapse before it's time to hit the shower.

Caveat

Since this type of running is the kind people seem to find most pleasant, it is a good time to prepare in other ways for the more strenuous training ahead. Elite runners, the ones who do not generally find themselves with any particular weight problem, might find this a good time to build up something of a "cushion" which will stand them in good stead later on when the stress of the daily routine actually makes it difficult to get enough in the way of nutrition.[55] This is a good time for such runners to eat as much as they want and to take supplemental vitamins in order to stave off colds and other nagging illnesses which interfere with training.

The psychology of Phase One training is important. The runner should think of himself or herself as a kind of thoroughbred disguised as a plow horse. It is far too early to give yourself away by running fast; the idea is to plod along, build up the odds, and get yourself mentally ready to run the fast races you know you will someday run. During this phase of training, I don't mind wearing bulky socks, heavier shoes, sweat tops, etc., because I know it doesn't matter if I feel, look, or run fast at this time of the year. For those of us on a normal distance runner's competitive schedule, this Phase One training usually starts in the fall and goes on through the colder months of the year, so getting into the psychology of the plodder is not too hard to do. This is a good time for meditation, for dreaming of spring and summer, of fast races on the roads or tracks.

But runners beware. The womblike serenity of Phase One has trapped many a runner. Hypnotized by the simplicity and relative ease of the one long, easy run per day, they put off what they know they must do if they would win races. They remain in Phase One and become what some call "training rats" or "distance bums," destined to extract whatever glory they can not from races, but from cocktail parties and taverns where they gloat over their mileage charts.

Just remember this: No one ever won the olive wreath with an impressive training diary.

PHASE TWO: A BREAK IN THE COCOON

This training, which lasts only three weeks, is actually a transition from the strict overdistance regimen of Phase

One to the mixture of intervals and faster overdistance of Phase Three. The overall mileage the runners cover every week will not change much, but the quality of a week's work will improve rather substantially.

From a superficial standpoint, it might not look like there is much change in the daily routine. This is especially true when you consider that from a strictly numerical standpoint, only 10 percent of the runner's total mileage is devoted to anything at all different from what he or she was doing in Phase One. But what a difference that 10 percent will make!

Once a week the runner will do a hill workout, springing up the inclines at a rather slow pace, concentrating on knee lift and stretching the leg muscles out for faster running later on. On one other day during the week, a session of long, relatively faster (but still slower than racing pace) intervals will mark the only other change in the regimen. The runner still continues the long run on Saturday or Sunday, and the other days continues the normal training regimen of one long run per day.

The runner will notice that, almost without any effort whatsoever, his pace on long runs will drop a minute a mile or more! This will be despite the runner's own efforts to keep the pace even and slow.

Such will be the improvement in normal pacing that the runner will be anxious to move on to the next step very quickly. Thus, this transitional hill and interval phase lasts only three weeks.

Purpose

The runner can expect six weeks of Phase One training to get much of the desired cellular work done. The mitochondria will have grown, the network of capillaries will have blossomed, the heart will have increased in size and stroke volume.

But the muscles themselves will not have been put to much

of a test as of yet. After all, the slow pace required on the long runs will have only exercised the aerobic, or slow-twitch muscles, leaving the anaerobic, or sprinting, muscles dormant. (If the runner wants to test this idea, he should wait until he is running between 70 and 100 miles per week—i.e., is "in shape"—and then go play an afternoon of sandlot basketball. The next day his sprinting muscles, his jumping muscles, and the rest of his anaerobic system will scarcely allow him to hobble around without the constant reminder that he may be "in shape" to run 10 miles a day, but that the Boston Celtics can still run circles around him on the hardwood.)

So it is that a transitional phase is necessary to begin preparing the muscles for some of the anaerobic work ahead. The hill work is geared toward stretching and strengthening primarily the upper thigh muscles called the quadriceps, whereas the light interval workout will help prepare the anaerobic pathways for the more strenuous interval workouts of Phase Three.

Length of Phase Two

Three weeks is desirable. If the runner is condensing his or her training in order to peak for a big race, this transitional phase is usually the one that gets squeezed or eliminated. Experienced runners can generally merge Phase One training right into Phase Three, but the less experienced runner takes a much higher chance of incurring injuries by leaving out this important bridge between long slow training and long fast training.

What Phase Two Does For You

The runner will emerge from three weeks of Phase Two with even better cellular and capillary development (remember, the mileage has been kept up, while the overall quality of training has also been improved). He or she can also expect to see much mechanical improvement in the running stride itself, particularly when running at faster speeds. This is due to the more flexible and more powerful muscles of the quadriceps beginning to play a more important role in the stride, due to hill training and light intervals.

In general, Phase Two gets the runner ready for the most important and most difficult of all training, the combination of intervals and overdistance of Phase Three.

Injury Strategy

Some readers might be surprised to find that there are runners scattered about the world who adhere strictly to the Lydiard system and thus are fanatical about their hillwork phase to the extent that they create somewhat of a spectacle in their training. Since Lydiard teaches that running *uphill* is highly beneficial during this phase of training, but that running *downhill* can cause injuries, there are runners who spring like drunken gazelles to the top of local hilltops, only to be solemnly driven down to the bottom again in automobiles by long-suffering and occasionally grim relatives or coaches.

You are not expected to ask that much of your probably already much-put-out friends and spouses, but you would be well advised to heed this warning: Running downhill is very hard on the body. If you live in an area not provided with trolley cars, you would be well advised to descend gently.

The penalties for doing otherwise include shin splints, puffy knees, sore hip joints, and foot ailments too numerous (and—unless they are your own—too boring) to mention.

How To Go About It

Lydiard recommends finding a hill at least 300 yards long, which rises one foot for every three horizontal feet. He also likes to find hills that have flat areas at the top and bottom for sprint work in between sessions of bouncing or springing up the gradient.[56]

In the best of all possible worlds, the hill would be a part of a circuit, with the return downhill portion at a less steep incline in order to make it easier on the leg muscles while descending.

Although specific workouts can be found in the charts beginning on page 119, the basics of the workout are quite simple. The runner springs up the hill in slow, bouncy strides, concentrating on form and stride, loosening and strengthening the quadriceps and calves. At the top of the hill, the runner jogs slowly, allowing the recovery which comes with dispersing lactic acid and replenishing glycogen to take place. He then runs the gentle downhill portion at a relatively fast pace, allowing the speed of the stride to further disperse the lactates. At the bottom of the hill, after four or five repetitions up the hill, the runner should do two to three "wind-sprint"-type intervals of varying distances, from 50 to 400 yards, in order to begin getting the body ready for the anaerobic work which will come later in training.

It should be noted at this point that the hill-training part of Phase Two is strenuous indeed, and the runner should not be surprised to find that he or she has inadvertently overdone it on the first day. The quadriceps and muscles in the buttocks particularly will be painful after the initial shock of the first session. The runner is advised to take it very easy until this new territory is explored fully. For instance, once you have located your hill circuit, you would be well advised to do only one set of four or five repetitions up the hill, with perhaps 10 × 110 wind sprints at the bottom to finish off, followed by several miles of light jogging. Even a "light" workout such as that might produce some soreness over the next several days (don't forget the Two-Day-Lag Rule).

As has been mentioned, the runner *must* learn his or her

own body and listen to its messages. Training time lost due to overall soreness and overtraining is no particular badge of honor among distance runners; it is more generally looked upon as naiveté, lack of insight, or just plain stupidity. Nobody cares that you lost the race because you missed a week of training with soreness or injuries that might well have been prevented. There is no slot in which to deposit your excuses and alibis at the finish line.

Caveats

It is very easy to allow overall mileage to slip once the runner begins programming hill work or intervals into his or her program. It is important that this not happen to any great extent. The runner should be concentrating on keeping total weekly mileage at about the same level in order to be assured that the aerobic cellular development continues apace while the muscles and the anaerobic pathways are being prepared for racing. In short, even though the more strenuous hill work and light interval session twice a week will increase the overall quality of the weekly mileage, the runner strives for the same quantity nonetheless. The body is quite capable of adapting to the increasing stress the runner is placing on it. As a matter of fact, that is precisely the name of this game: getting racing fit.

PHASE THREE: THE BUTTERFLY EMERGES

This is where the real business of becoming racing fit is carried on. It is a combination of overdistance (which is becoming quite a bit faster-paced by now) and rather bulky interval workouts at paces approaching what the runner will expect from himself or herself during a race. The rest portion of the interval workouts, however, will still be somewhat merciful, generally consisting of jogging the same distance as the repetition just completed.

This is the phase at which those runners who compete at a high level all year round tend to stay. Many who do not adhere to the One Big Race school consider Phase Three training to be the only kind there is. And for those who take no real "vacation" from running, for those who do not go for the ultimate "peak" every year (which necessitates starting all over with the "base" building period), Phase Three training *is* the only kind of training there is. They don't need to worry about going back aind starting on long gentle ten-mile runs. They don't need to do three weeks on the hills. They don't need to begin gently working into intervals.

Basically, their training is exactly where they want it to be: high quality and high quantity. The national and world-class athletes maintaining this type of training for the better part of the year will be putting in 85 to 130 miles per week including two tough interval sessions during the week and a pretty quick 15-to-20-miler on Sunday. Of such cloth champions are cut—if they can last, physically and mentally, at that level.

All that is necessary to get ready for a quasi-peak performance is to lower the intensity of the work for a week or more, sharpen the quality of the interval work (while shortening the rest periods), and then schedule several very light days before the competition.

Presto: the quasi-peak! The benefits of this approach are obvious. If the runner is willing to undergo the pressure of such constant quality and quantity in his or her training, then the high-level performance is never really far away. The runner simply carries on the routine day in and day out, picks the races to shoot for, and then plans the easing-off period accordingly. The trophy goes on the shelf Saturday night, and Monday morning bright and early the whole process begins all over again.

Purpose

By combining overdistance training and interval training, the runner is preparing both aerobically and anaerobically to undergo the ultimate stress of the race. If the runner is prepared only in the aerobic phase, then the runner will be beaten by those who can sustain a faster pace or who can outsprint him or her to the finish. If the runner is prepared only anaerobically, he or she will be ready to sprint like a cheetah at the beginning and the end of the race, but he will win nothing because distance races are not won by those who can sprint short distances unless they can also hang on during the interminable middle laps or miles.

Thus Phase Three training is designed to put it all together: to develop the complete racing machine.

Length of Phase

For the runner on the six-month program, this phase will last six weeks; for the runner on the year program, twelve weeks. For the runner who wishes to train and race at a high level year round, this phase is interminable, until injury interrupts, or until the Big Race finally rolls around and the runner goes into the Phase Four peaking process.

What Phase Three Does for You

In a word, everything. If the runner were fit enough to walk out the first day and begin training at Phase Three, that would be ideal, because this level of training is the most efficient, most beneficial, most well-rounded of all. Although there is the constant danger of injury or staleness (overtraining) because of the quality of the work performed, there is also the constant joy of knowing that a very-high-quality competitive performance is but a few days rest away at any given time.

The overdistance is more than sufficient to keep developing the cellular capabilities to their utmost, the heart will continue to enlarge itself until limiting factors we can only guess at (chest cavity size?) decree an end to the process, and the capillary network will become a miracle of a delivery system. In short, the aerobic system will be operating like a dynamo.

Meanwhile, the twice-weekly interval workouts on the track or grass field will have the fast-twitch muscles ready to deliver their quick bursts of speed when called upon, and the fast-red fibers will have been training to keep up the "floating"-type sprint necessary to win half-mile or mile races (which are, these days, little more than semisprints most of the way).

Phase Three puts it all together.

Injury Strategy

At no other time in training is it more important to watch for injuries or illness. Since the earlier phases involve less overall stress on the body, and since by Phase Four one would expect the body to have already reacted by injury or illness if it were going to, Phase Three training is the real culprit on down time.

I occasionlly refer to the mental and physical condition of this phase as "the valley of fatigue" because the demands that are placed on the body are enormous and it is often quite difficult to find enough rest between workouts to recover sufficiently. It is during this phase that the runner who is so dedicated as to take only a part-time job (or who, through scholarship, hook, or crook, doesn't have to work at all) will truly surpass the runner who tries to lead the dual life of a nine-to-fiver and a twice-a-day runner.

It is also quite easy to overtrain during this phase, since the runner will be trying to maintain mileage while increasing the overall quality of his workouts tremendously with the double dose of hard intervals during the week. This is sometimes referred to as "breaking down."

Obviously it is far better not to push oneself to that point, but it is often difficult to avoid. The body by this point has become so hardened, and the Two-Day-Lag Rule being what it is, the runner will find it difficult to tell when he is overdoing it.

That is precisely the reason one keeps an accurate calendar, listens to the subtle messages the body is constantly sending, and heeds the various warning signs when they appear. Although one wants to keep training at a high level during this period, particular attention should be paid to injuries that don't "go away" or to such things as sore throats, which may be harbingers of worse things to come. The runner's resistance will often be low during this phase, and it is recommended particularly at this time that he or she take supplemental nutrients as recommended earlier.

The great miler and half-miler Peter Snell, Lydiard's most famous runner, records his own thoughts about mixing this phase of training with fairly serious competition:

> I had been competing at high pressure for about six months and, according to my pattern, I was reaching the point where my body would be entering a natural depression in training performance. I was on the brink of the inevitable abyss. This is both mental and physical. Mentally, it's very hard to continue the pressure of training and, if you ignore these warning signs, it's very easy to go down with flu or some similar upset which forces you to have the lay-off you need.[57]

One important point worth making again is the athlete's self-knowledge. Snell knew very well from his own experience what he would be going through, as well as the penalty he would pay if he did not heed the warning signs. All good runners who last for more than a few races are usually magicians at figuring out what was going on inside their own musculature and psyche. A reading of the biographies of almost any of the great runners of the past will show this to be true. The runner *must* be aware of the injury dangers of this particular phase of training, and if necessary begin practicing the fine art of "quiet hypochondria," which simply means that you may need to strap an icepack to a sore knee, but you don't necessarily have to tell everyone about it.

How To Go About It

The overall mileage should remain at approximately the level established toward the middle of the Phase One training, but of course the quality will be improving markedly.

At this stage both the morning runs and the long afternoon runs should be considered almost "recovery" runs. They won't be jogging by any means (as a matter of fact, they will be considerably faster than at any earlier stage), but they will be fairly easy compared to the real work which takes place during this phase: the interval sessions.

But don't make the mistake one 3:57 miler I knew used to make. When he got into Phase Three training one year he ran the interval workouts with the milers on alternate days, then on the "off days" instead of running their normally paced overdistance runs, he attempted to work out with the three- and six-milers as they did much faster overdistance. In short, he was trying to match the "quality" work of both groups simultaneously. He was lucky to have lasted the season.

It is far better to train with one group and keep everyone "in synch" with each other. Just skipping one morning workout can make a big difference as to who feels spry in the afternoon and who doesn't. Such fatigue gaps can lead to ill feelings (or worse).

The long run on Sunday now becomes optional. For one thing, the runner may now begin to look at competition more seriously. A race on Saturday should definitely *not* be followed by a strenuous 15- to-20-miler on Sunday. That would be asking the body to stretch itself too far between the aerobic base-building running on the one hand, and the competitive-level racing on the other. Far better to follow a serious race with a relatively easy ten-miler on Sunday. There is actually some degree of danger in overtraining during the rosy afterglow of a good racing effort.

During this phase the one hill-work session per week is abandoned in favor of an afternoon interval workout every other day. A typical afternoon's work might include (after several miles of warm-up and stride-outs) 12 quarter-miles with a quarter-mile jog rest for recovery; or possibly 20 × 220 with a 220 jog rest; or 16 × 330 with a 330 jog rest. For specific workouts, see the charts beginning on page 119.

These are what are called "in-and-out" intervals, which means that the rest recovery period is the same distance as the repetition. This allows for nearly complete recovery, i.e., the heart rate will come back relatively close to "resting" level. (By very close I mean within 10 to 15 beats of the base rate. If the runner does not achieve this rate during the recovery period, then it is not long enough and should be lengthened.)

Most runners are generally curious to know what kind of times are recommended for completion of each repetition. In setting times for their runners, coaches and experts in the past have gone to great lengths to explain their recommendations, basing them on the best "scientific" information available.

All that is basically unnecessary. I go by the axiom of training that Jumbo Elliot of Villanova used: KISS (Keep It Simple, Stupid).

With reference to interval times KISS means that one should run them slow enough on the first workout to be able to do them all comfortably. The next week when the runner does the same workout, he or she should simply try for a time a second or so faster. It's that easy. Over the course of the six weeks of Phase Three, the times should be dropping dramatically. Of course, they will drop more rapidly at the beginning than they will later on, as the runner gets close to the maximum of his or her abilities.

It is truly remarkable (even to elite runners) to see how quickly their interval times drop from one week to the next. For instance, every year when we begin to go into the "valley of fatigue" of Phase Three training, our quarter-mile efforts will almost always be in the 67-to-72-second range, depending upon conditions. And they will seem as difficult as if we were trying to run them in 57 or 58 seconds.

After several weeks, the aerobic pathways will be working much better, our sprinting muscles will be getting much more tone, and we will be much more comfortable with this faster-paced running. And inevitably—even with the same effort as we put forth in the beginning of the phase—we will see our times drop to the 59-to-62-second range, or even lower.

What the runner must keep in mind in the beginning of such a phase of training is precisely that: Things *will* get easier. There is not an elite runner in the world who has not been regularly amazed to find out how hard that first session of 70-second quarters seems—when he had been running 59s only four months earlier!

Thus, the answer to that question we hear in every running clinic—"How fast should we do our intervals?"—is simply this: Do them as fast as you can and still get them *all* done during your normal workout time. Then proceed every week to try to improve, a little at a time. To put it in terms of sheer numbers, if a Category C runner is starting out by running 8 × 440 in about 80 seconds each the first week, the second week he or she should be trying to hit somewhere about 78 or 79. By the end of Phase Three training, that same runner might well be running at close to 70 seconds or better. The Category A runner will be close to 60 seconds or better. The very best milers and three-milers will all then be running well under 60 seconds for 10 or 12 quarter-miles.

It is important for the coach or the self-coached runner not to try to start with too difficult a standard. In other words, the runner should not be struggling during that first workout in order that he or she can brag about the times accomplished. That will only lead to a very rapid "break-down" situation and the runner will be extremely disappointed to find his or her times going *up* the next week, not down.

It is for this reason that I very rarely time early-season interval workouts. I run them on a big grass field in Gainesville without a watch, trusting my own internal clock to keep on pace. I am much more concerned with keeping the "effort" at a high level than I am with my times.

I save early-season timed track workouts as little "treats," when I would put on spikes and allow myself to be tested against the unforgiving stopwatch. I set goals during these workouts that I am fairly confident I can achieve, and thus am always pleasantly surprised when the times come out a bit faster than I "expected." Just another little ploy to make the game interesting.

One important psychological difference between Phase Three and the earlier two phases is that this is the first time the runner will consciously be pushing him or herself in most of the workouts. The effort involved in trying to meet the interval times established prior to the workout will be noticeable. This doesn't mean that such goals aren't subject to amendment if the athlete is having difficulty achieving them (after all, even a slight wind may affect a runner's ability to keep to his or her predetermined schedule), but that there will be real striving to meet those objectives for the first time.

Such an attitude is in marked contrast to the easy paces of Phase One training, and the gentle hill springing and short "wind sprints" of Phase Two training. The runner may perhaps find him- or herself needing to "get psyched" before a workout; indeed, as the times get faster, it will almost be required. A quality interval workout cannot, in fact, be run by someone whose mind is elsewhere.

The runner must keep in mind that one of the goals of this type of training is to build up the leg speed so that racing pace (or a bit faster than racing pace) is manageable for some distance with relative comfort. Both stride and muscle tone will be greatly enhanced by the end of this phase, which means that running speeds will have improved markedly for *all* distances, short and long.

It is toward the end of this phase that the runner should find himself or herself at optimum racing weight. If for some reason extra weight is flapping around here and there, something is wrong. Conversely, if the runner's body has not received adequate nutrition during this strenuous period, it is also quite possible for even the finely honed runner to be quite malnourished (and thus susceptible to illness).[58]

Though the interval workouts will be quite difficult, the runner should never try to simulate the actual lactic acid buildup of racing conditions. He or she should stay well within himself or herself, never truly straining at the end, never using the "afterburners." The runner can usually tell when he or she is "straining" more than "training." The use of the arms in pumping through the last 100 yards is a dead giveaway of "straining." When he is able to use them smoothly, flowing through the end of the interval without frantic pumping, then he is still "training." It is a matter of control, of cadence. The general rule in this phase is: Know Thyself; and then Stay Within Thyself.

When the going gets tough (as it always does during this phase), the runner must keep in mind that it is, in fact, the hardest training of the entire year. Though not as long as Phase One, it is much more *intense*. It sometimes seems as though it will never end. For the college runner on a year-long training program, it is long indeed, lasting from approximately December to June.

Caveats

As mentioned above, Phase Three training is grueling. It is the time most runners will begin to develop overuse injuries. It is therefore a time when the runner must become something of a hypochondriac and treat all injuries with the same loving attention. Every nagging ache and pain might develop into a debilitating (and psychologically devastating) roadblock.

It is also a dangerous time for overtraining, or "breaking down." For runners who begin to show the symptoms (as described in Chapter Five), I would heartily recommend an immediate blood test. If the test shows signs of anemia (brought on by the destruction of red blood cells caused by severe training), the runner will have to take some time off. There is simply no way around it; to continue to train under such circumstances is to court injury or illness. And, as the indomitable Snell previously remarked, such a reaction is your body's way of getting a message to you which you had been trying to ignore: "If you ignore these warning signs, it's very easy to go down with flu or some similar upset *which forces you to have the lay-off you need*" (emphasis added).

One final, very general comment about the psychology of the individual interval workout itself. It almost always follows the same pattern, which is that the first 25 percent of the workout seems very easy, but at the halfway point you begin to wonder if you can make it at all. Then the last two repetitions seem relatively easy again. Most of it is psychology. It requires experience, confidence, and mental toughness to handle this kind of training with any real consistency. If you find yourself dreading the afternoon's prospects like the fires of the netherworld, then it is quite possible you are overdoing it, and would do well to compromise with an easy overdistance run until the following day.

But it has been my experience that much of this dread comes from the "valley of fatigue" gloom and not from any real physical problems. Occasionally such workouts—though I may have dreaded them throughout the morning—turn out to be some of the best training performances I have ever turned in.

That brings to mind one of the most perplexing ironies in all of distance running, and that is the very rare (usually *very* talented) elite runner who actually gets psychologically trapped in *this* phase of training and thus becomes what might be called a "superior" training rat.

He or she goes through week after week of absolutely astounding Phase Three training, "running through" all competition with abandon, generally doing quite well in those races but never quite working himself or herself up to the ultimate peak. I am speaking of runners (I know several) who have run under 2:20 for the marathon, under 4:00 for the mile, who—though they can match their world-class peers in Phase Three training—are still unable to move from that training to that zenith of conditioning necessary to run "that One Big Race" everyone knows they have within themselves.

In short, they don't understand the crucial Phase Four training which allows every runner who has prepared himself or herself to step out onto the road or track one sunny day . . . and run the race of a lifetime.

PHASE FOUR: THE BUTTERFLY TAKES FLIGHT

This last, very short, very intense period of training is the one that seems to elude even the most experienced elite runners at times. Having gone through literally years of training to prepare the body for a big race, the runner suddenly realizes as the big day approaches that he or she doesn't know exactly what to do to put that last little fine edge on the blade. Should you stop running altogether and just rest? Should you train even harder, trying to use the last several weeks of stress to push the body into new frontiers of condition? Should you just run long overdistance to keep the aerobic pathways open, but avoid the lactic acid buildup of interval work?

These are puzzling questions indeed, and over the years they have been debated back and forth by even the very best competitive runners.

Arthur Lydiard, once again, came along to point the way for the rest of us. Here is what he has to say about this last all-important phase of training:

> You should train every day during this period, but well within your capabilities. If you use fast running, it should be short and intense, not prolonged. The longer runs should be made at an easy pace. Watch your food intake during this time. There can be a tendency to ease up in training and overeat. It is not desirable to put on any weight. So if you are susceptible to weight gain, take particular care.[59]

Purpose

Phase Four is designed to simulate racing conditions in workouts and thus to bring all the body's physiological mechanisms to their absolute peak. No longer will the runner be concerned with muscle tone, aerobic and anaerobic pathways, flexibility, etc. He or she will be more concerned with getting plenty of rest between these lighter, shorter but more intense intervals of "speed" workouts. He or she will be concerned with the nuances of racing, such as the fluidity of the stride at fast racing speeds. He or she will use this period to enhance strengths, to bolster weaknesses. If he or she expects to race against competitors who surge, he or she will practice surge training. If he or she expects to run against front-runners, he or she will need to work on relentless pace work.

The workouts themselves will still be interval-type sessions (alternating with long, easy overdistance when necessary), but they will be faster, more condensed than the intervals of Phase Three. Nearly all sessions will be timed, and the runner will run the repetitions as if racing. Instead of 12 × 440 in 62, the elite runner will now try to do 6 in 57.

The rest/recovery period will also be different. The runner is no longer jogging between repetitions to disperse the lactic acid. Instead, in order to simulate racing conditions where the lactic acid will remain at a fairly high state (except during the very longest races), the runner will take only a short rest, and will walk instead of jog. Thus, he or she will be beginning each repetition with at least a partial lactic acid buildup.

After even as little as a week's worth of such work, the runner will notice that he or she is "coming around." The "valley of fatigue" sluggishness of the previous phase will be gone. The runner will be more rested, more alert. The runner will feel an almost "itchy" sensation, a desire to get out and run fast at almost any time of day or night. It is quite unlike any other sensation I have ever known, and it is difficult indeed to convey.

What Phase Four Does For You

It simply gets you ready to race at your physical and mental peak. It puts the final tone on already hardened muscles and perfects the functioning of the anaerobic pathways. It also perfects the fluidity of the stride at racing speeds.

Injury Strategy

This phase of training does not generally generate injury problems. For one thing, the runner has more energy, is more alert. The stride is light, fast, and bouncy. There is very little "slogging" through workouts, as there occasionally was in Phase Three training. Thus, it is not an injury-prone time. Perhaps the biggest danger during this phase is the runner's abundance of energy. Occasionally a competitor, overwhelmed with this sudden exuberance which was not available in previous training phases, will feel like going out and "hitting the old tennis ball" or "playing a little flag football with the boys." That is a trap to be avoided at all costs. The snapped ankle or twisted knee incurred by such shenanigans make an afternoon's frolic a poor substitute for the victory which you worked so long and hard for.

Far better to save your enthusiasm for picnic sports for the off-season, or until such time as you hang up your racing shoes for good.

How to Go About It

Specific workouts can be found in the charts beginning on page 119, but in general the runner will be on the track at least every other day, in spikes or light flats. The workouts will consist of intervals as in Phase Three, but the runner will generally do about half the number. They will be very "sharp," i.e., the runner will be running close to all-out for many of them. This is the time to go to the afterburners, to reach down and pull out the last bit of speed over the last 50 yards, to pump the arms and to imagine you are in a racing situation. This is the one time it is permissible to race your fellows a bit and test each others' strength.

The rest/recovery interval will be much different. The runner will walk around for a short period of time between repetitions, not trying to recover, but merely to get his or her breath back. The legs will still be heavy with lactic acid when the new repetition is begun, but that is exactly what is wanted: a simulation of the racing experience. The heart will develop its top-end capabilities during this phase. After growing both larger and stronger during the earlier training, it will now be pushed to its limits during the very short interval-recovery periods as it tries to flush the lactic acid out of the laboring muscle cells. This is extremely important because the heart will be called upon to labor at its absolute physical peak during the final stages of a distance race, the last 300 yards or so, as the runner calls upon it for the last bit of speed he or she can muster. This racing peak is developed in Phase Four workouts simply by keeping that heart rate elevated to its top-end capabilities for much longer periods than it will experience in a race. The last 300 yards of a fast mile race may take only 40 seconds or so, but in a Phase Four interval workout the heart will be forced to remain at that level for as long as eight to ten minutes, when all the repetitions are added up.

The importance of this heart work is best exemplified by the cases of Villanova miler Dave Patrick and former world record holder Jim Ryun. Neither had a truly impressive low base heart rate (they were in the high 50s, low 60s), but both could get up over 220 at the top end, and both were superior last-lap competitors. They both had a very high cardiac output (the total number of liters of blood pumped by the heart per minute).

The workouts at this time are simplicity itself: very condensed, very fast, very short rest breaks, followed by four to eight miles of light jogging to aid in recovery. The workout might be composed of 8 × 440; or 12 × 220; or 5 × 880; or combinations of different distances called "step-downs." It really makes very little difference so long as the result is achieved.

Mileage at this stage of the season becomes almost irrelevant. It will generally drop to about 75 percent of the former totals to allow for the more intense work. The runner might spend as much as five days of the week on the track, but not every workout will necessarily be of the same intensity as all the rest. The runner will aways start off the workout with at least 8 × 110 "striders" or wind sprints. Some runners have been known to do an entire workout of 110 sprints, several miles of them altogether!

Group training is helpful during this phase, as it teaches the runner to run fast in a pack and will keep the competitive juices flowing. In terms of quality, these workouts will be the very best running the competitor can produce short of races themselves.

But psychologically these workouts will be much harder than races for the simple reason that they will last longer. Thus it is necessary for the runner to "get psyched" in order to perform well at this stage of training.

The runner will probably want to continue running twice a day, using the morning workout as a time to keep up his or her aerobic conditioning and to flush the lactic acid from the previous afternoon's exertions. The morning workout will help the runner loosen up for the afternoon session.

Caveats

Once you're in this phase, you've stepped over the line and are on your way to peaking. It is difficult indeed to go back to any previous phase. The runner will be racing fit for as long as four to six weeks with very little more than light jogging and occasional wind sprints after the completion of this phase. It is very important for the competitor to keep racing regularly in order to maintain this edge, and if no races are available, he or she should do time trials. The Lydiard rule of thumb is at least two competitions per week, whether time trial or race.

Many runners have difficulty with this concept, and after several weeks of racing and little else they get nervous about their condition. They want to bolster their flagging confidence (which, after all, derives from their miles and miles of logged training—and which they don't get while in the racing phase) by going out and running hard workouts. What they generally find is that it is next to impossible to run a good-quality interval workout as they did in Phase Three. They have simply gone beyond that point and will need to go back to Phase One and rebuild their base before they will be able to handle those long, stressful intervals.

It's all psychological anyway. The race is what they have spent all that time and effort for; they really ought to relax and enjoy the peak for as long as it lasts.

When I spend the summer in Europe running races, I do little else but jog and sightsee. The first time I come into the last 440 and reach down for that reserve that should be there and find it isn't, that's when I start thinking about going home.

Several weeks (and pounds) later, the cool breezes of fall begin to remind the runner that it's nearly time to start the process all over again.

It's the eternal cycle of the runner's year, and I wouldn't trade it for anything.

Chart One

Categories of Runners

This very subjective classification will be helpful for the runner to decide what kind of workouts (intensity and duration) he or she ought to attempt. Reference is made in Chart 2 to the categories presented here, and in several places throughout the book a working knowledge of these competitive levels will prove helpful.

These breakdowns are to be used only as a general guide, however. Workout intensity is the most difficult single determination a coach or runner must make. One should always keep one's workout intentions flexible in order to avoid injury or overtraining.

One word of caution to females and runners younger than seventeen or older than thirty: For the purpose of determining the best workouts for you, choose the category that fits most closely, regardless of how you compare to your peers.

These categories have not been adjusted for age or sex, but are based strictly on ability. This leads to some aberrations. For instance, according to the charts, there are no world-class women milers, since no female has run under 4:10 for the mile. Such is clearly not the case, however. There *are* world-class women milers.

Women who wish to extrapolate their correct category in *relative* terms (i.e., when compared to other female runners) should make a rough comparison of world-record times for men and women for the three distances. Women should add approximately 30 seconds to the mile times, five minutes to the 10,000-meter times, and 22 minutes to the marathon times.

In other words, a woman with a best time in the mile of 4:59 would be classified as a Category A runner when compared to her peers. However, for the purposes of determining her workouts from this book, she should follow the Category B schedules.

WORLD-CLASS RUNNERS

TIMES:	Mile	under 4:10
	10,000	under 31:00
	Marathon	under 2:23

EXPERIENCE: At least six years of competitive running.

COMPETES: 10 to 20 times a year or more.

WEIGHT: Never a factor; probably has difficulty keeping weight on during hard training. World-class runners are generally 7 percent body fat or less, with the exception of some competitors in the shorter distances (5,000 meters or less).

MILEAGE: Some run less, but most in this category run at least 100 miles a week most of the year, sometimes 140 or even more.

CATEGORY A RUNNERS

TIMES:	Mile	under 4:30
	10,000	under 34:00
	Marathon	under 2:35

Experience: At least three years of competitive running, generally.

Competes: 10 to 20 times a year or more.

Weight: Usually 5 to 12 percent body fat; weight not usually a factor with this runner if training seriously.

Mileage: Probably runs or is capable of running in excess of 65 miles per week; many in this class, particularly older runners, will do 80 to 90 miles per week when training seriously.

CATEGORY B RUNNERS

Times:	Mile	under 5:00
	10,000	under 38:00
	Marathon	under 2:50

Experience: Probably running at least a year, but an athlete of this ability may well have participated in other sports before taking up running.

Competes: 5 to 10 times a year seriously, perhaps more races of the "fun run" type in addition.

Weight: Often a factor; this runner will often use training as a weight-control device simply because some of the larger physiques are found in this group.

Mileage: 35 to 65 a week.

CATEGORY C RUNNERS

Times:	Mile	under 6:00
	10,000 meters	under 45:00
	Marathon	under 3:20

Experience: Probably running competitively less than a year, and perhaps has had some earlier sports experience.

Competes: 5 to 10 times a year, generally at about the same competitive level.

WEIGHT: Often a factor; occasionally these runners will need to watch their diet in addition to keeping up training mileage to ensure racing success.

MILEAGE: 20 to 35 miles per week, sometimes less.

OTHERS

Runners and would-be runners who fit into none of the above categories have some preliminary work to do before this book can be of any real help. Although such runners may find the book useful, they need more basic advice to get them headed in the right direction. The Joe Henderson book cited in the notes is highly recommended for this purpose.

The following recommendations are also offered:

1. *Do not* attempt to follow the training system set out in this book as of yet.

2. *Do not* attempt to do interval training of any kind as of yet.

3. Take *at least* another six months of running and try to increase your daily mileage gradually, while following the general rules set out in Chapter 3, particularly the Consistency Ethic and the Two-Day-Lag Rule.

4. If you have a weight problem, use dieting in conjunction with your daily running to get it under control. No one with a weight problem can hope to do the training described in Chapter 4 successfully.

5. Come back in six months, or as soon as you find yourself in Category C. For older runners or for women, be sure to give yourself the extra time adjustments noted earlier.

6. Take heart. Neither Rome nor a swift body was built in a day.

Chart Two

Sample Workouts

ELITE RUNNERS

Phase One—Typical Week

Monday	A.M.	7 miles easy
	P.M.	8 miles at 7-minute pace, 2 miles of 110 striders (alternate a hard 110 with a 110 jog)
Tuesday	A.M.	5 miles easy
	P.M.	10 miles easy
Wednesday	A.M.	7 miles easy
	P.M.	10 miles easy
Thursday	A.M.	5 miles easy
	P.M.	12 miles easy
Friday	A.M.	8 miles easy
	P.M.	9 miles easy

Saturday	A.M.	5	miles easy
	P.M.	10	miles easy
Sunday	A.M. or P.M.	18	to 22 miles at 7-minute pace

Phase Two—Typical Week

Monday	A.M.	5	miles easy
	P.M.	10	miles easy
Tuesday	A.M.	5	miles easy
	P.M.		jog 3 miles, do 4 × 110 striders hard, alternating with a 110 jog in between, then 8 × 200 to 300 uphill, using slow bouncing stride going up, jog coming down. Finish with 4 × 110 easy striders
Wednesday	A.M.	7	miles easy
	P.M.	10	miles very easy
Thursday	A.M.	5	miles easy
	P.M.		jog 3 miles, 4 × 110 easy striders, then 4 × 400 to 600 uphill, then 4 × 100 easy striders, jog 2 miles warm-down
Friday	A.M.	5	miles easy
	P.M.	10	miles very easy
Saturday	A.M.	3	miles easy
	P.M.		jog 3 miles, 4 × 200 to 300 uphill, then 4 to 8 × 330 on grass field or track w/110 jog recovery
Sunday	A.M. or P.M.	15	to 20 miles at 7-minute pace

Phase Three—Typical Week

Monday	A.M.	5	miles easy
	P.M.		jog 3 miles, 8 × 110 striders, 10 to 15 × 440 @ 72-second pace w/440 jog recovery, 3-mile warmdown
Tuesday	A.M.	7	miles easy
	P.M.	10	miles easy
Wednesday	A.M.	5	miles easy
	P.M.		jog 3 miles, 8 × 110 striders, 16 to 20 × 220 @ 33-second pace w/220 jog recovery, 3-mile warmdown
Thursday	A.M.	7	miles easy
	P.M.	10	miles easy
Friday	A.M.	3	miles easy
	P.M.	10	miles brisk
Saturday	A.M. or P.M.		race or easy time trial, or a long interval-type workout, such as 8 × 660 @ 1:50 w/330 jog, 3-mile warmdown
Sunday	A.M. or P.M.	10	to 15 miles easy

Phase Four—Last Two Weeks

Monday	A.M.	3	miles easy
	P.M.		jog 2 miles, 8 × 110, then do two sets of the following: 1 × 220 @ 30, 1 × 440 @ 60, 1 × 660 @ 1:30, 1 × 440 @ 60, 1 × 220 @ 29. Note that pace is constant, only distance

			varies. Recovery between intervals is only *60 seconds*! Recovery between sets is complete. *Always* warm down with 2 or 3 easy miles
Tuesday	A.M.	5	miles easy
	P.M.	10	miles easy
Wednesday	A.M.	3	miles easy
	P.M.		jog 3 miles, 8 × 110, 2 miles at 80 percent effort on track for time (for elite runners this may range from 9:00 to 9:50, depending on fatigue from earlier workouts. The *effort* is the important factor)
Thursday	A.M.	5	miles easy
	P.M.		jog 3 miles, 8 × 110 easy, 5 miles easy
Friday	A.M.	5	miles easy
	P.M.		jog 2 miles, 8 × 110, 10 × 440 @ 58 to 63 seconds, w/60-second recovery
Saturday	A.M.	10	miles good pace
Sunday	A.M. or P.M.	15	to 18 miles easy
Monday	A.M.	5	miles easy
	P.M.		jog 2 miles, 8 × 110, 2 miles of "surges" (sprinting 50, jogging 60), keeping time for total distance
Tuesday	A.M.	5	miles easy
	P.M.		jog 2 miles, 8 × 110, 660 brisk, floating stride, rest 30 seconds, 220

		hard, jog 880, repeat 4 times. In standard notation: 4 × (660 hard w/30 sec., 220 hard, w/30 sec.) w/ 880 jog between sets, 2 miles warmdown
Wednesday	A.M.	3 miles easy
	P.M.	8 miles easy
Thursday	A.M.	3 miles easy
	P.M.	jog 2 miles, 8 × 110, 10 × 220 medium hard, w/220 jog, 2 miles warmdown
Friday	A.M.	5 miles easy
	P.M.	10 miles easy
Saturday	A.M.	5 miles easy
	P.M.	jog 2 miles, then 660, 550, 440, 330, all easy pace with 440 jog recovery, then 3 × 150 slow, medium, hard, jog 440, then 4 × 440 at racing pace, w/220 jog recovery
Sunday	A.M. or P.M.	12 to 15 miles easy

CATEGORY A RUNNERS

Phase One—Typical Week

Monday	A.M.	3 miles easy
	P.M.	4 miles, 8 × 110 easy
Tuesday	A.M. or P.M.	10 miles

Wednesday	A.M. or P.M.	12	miles
Thursday	A.M.	3	miles easy
	P.M.	10	miles
Friday		10	miles
Saturday		8	miles, run middle 6 briskly
Sunday		12	to 15 miles

Phase Two—Typical Week

Monday	A.M.	3	miles easy
	P.M.	5	miles
Tuesday	P.M.		jog 3 miles, 4 × 110, 4 × 220 to 300 hill or stadium steps, 4 × 110 striders, 2 miles easy warmdown
Wednesday	A.M. or P.M.	10	miles easy
Thursday	A.M.	8	miles fartlek run, preferably on hilly terrain
Friday		12	miles easy
Saturday			race or fast 5-mile run
Sunday			12 to 15 on flat ground

Phase Three—Typical Week

Monday	P.M.		jog 3 miles, 6-10 × 440 at race pace w/440 jog
Tuesday		12	miles easy

Wednesday	P.M.		jog 3 miles, 10-16 x 220 at race pace w/220 jog
Thursday		10	miles easy
Friday			jog 3 miles, 4 × 880 @ easy pace w/880 jog, 2 mile warmdown
Saturday		8	miles easy
Sunday		12	to 15 miles easy

Phase Four—Typical Week

Monday	P.M.		jog 3 miles, 8 × 110 striders, 1 × (220, 440, 440, 220) all @ racing pace, all w/60-second rest
Tuesday		8	miles easy
Wednesday			jog 3 miles, 8 × 110 striders, 8 × 440 @ racing pace w/220 jog
Thursday			jog 3 miles, 8 × 110 striders, 2 miles of 50-60s ("surge training," sprint 50, then jog 60 yards)
Friday		6	miles easy
Saturday			race or time trial
Sunday		10	miles easy

CATEGORY B RUNNERS

Phase One—Typical Week

Monday		6	miles easy, 8 × 110 striders
Tuesday	A.M.	4	miles easy
	P.M.	8	miles easy

Wednesday	A.M. or P.M.	8 miles easy
Thursday		5 miles easy
Friday		8 miles easy
Saturday		3 miles at hard pace
Sunday		8 to 12 miles easy

Phase Two—Typical Week

Monday	5 miles easy
Tuesday	jog 1 mile, 4 × 200 to 300 uphill, jog down, 4 × 110 striders on flat ground, jog 1 mile warmdown
Wednesday	5 miles easy
Thursday	5 to 8 miles easy
Friday	jog 1 mile, 4 × 300 to 400 uphill, jog 1 mile warmdown
Saturday	5 miles easy
Sunday	8 to 10 miles easy

Phase Three—Typical Week

Monday	jog 1 mile, 8 × 110, 8 × 440 w/440 jog @ racing pace
Tuesday	5 miles easy
Wednesday	8 miles easy
Thursday	jog 1 mile, 10 × 220 at racing pace, 220 jog recovery, 1 mile warmdown

Friday	4 miles easy
Saturday	3 miles fast or race
Sunday	8 to 12 miles easy

Phase Four—Typical Week

Monday	3 to 5 miles easy
Tuesday	jog 1 mile, 1½ miles @ racing pace, 1 mile warmdown
Wednesday	5 miles easy
Thursday	jog 1 mile, 2 miles of 50-60s (sprint 50, jog 60) on track, 1 mile warmdown
Friday	3 miles easy
Saturday	race
Sunday	8 miles easy

CATEGORY C RUNNERS

Phase One—Typical Week

Monday	2 to 4 miles easy
Tuesday	4 to 6 miles easy
Wednesday	2 to 4 miles easy
Thursday	2 to 4 miles easy
Friday	2 to 4 miles easy
Saturday	recovery day
Sunday	6 to 10 miles easy

Phase Two—Typical Week

Monday	3 miles on hilly course
Tuesday	jog 3 to 5 miles
Wednesday	4 to 6 miles easy
Thursday	4 to 6 miles on hilly course
Friday	3 miles easy
Saturday	recovery day
Sunday	6 to 10 miles easy

Phase Three—Typical Week

Monday	jog 1 mile, 4 × 880 striders, 1 × 880 at racing pace, 1 mile warm-down
Tuesday	4 miles easy
Wednesday	jog 1 mile, 4 × 110 striders, 4 × 440 @ racing pace w/440 jog
Thursday	4 to 6 miles easy
Friday	3 miles easy
Saturday	race or hard 3 miles
Sunday	8 to 12 miles

Phase Four

I do not recommend that Category C runners attempt peaking training per se. Rather, when preparing for a big race, such runners should take at least three easy days before competition and should moderate or eliminate the Wednesday interval workout the week before the race.

Chapter Five

The Injuries

It is impossible to overemphasize the importance of injury prevention and treatment to the career of a successful athlete. It has often been noted that the champion athlete is very often one who has attained a high level of lay expertise and downright craftiness with regard to injuries, whereas novices seem to keep getting hurt.[60]

Very often the difference between the perennial champion and the perennial bridesmaid is just that edge: an ability to avoid and/or recover quickly from physical trauma.

Once again, the runner will need to be self-reliant. The venerable gray-haired family physician who brought you into the world and guided you through chicken pox and worse will be of little use to you in this area (unless he or she happens to also be a marathoner—which is more and more a possibility these days). The traditional medical response to overuse injuries and athletic problems of all types has been: stay off it. That, naturally, will not do.

There are some injuries which will necessitate total rest,

of course. But many can be treated while continuing to train, sometimes in a modified form. Others can be rested while the athlete undertakes alternative training methods such as cycling or swimming.

The runner will need to become a student of the subject, which involves far more detailed information than is possible in this summary. For that reason, I recommend the excellent *The Sportsmedicine Book*, written by Dr. Gabe Mirkin (a long-time competitive runner).

It is possible, however, to give some guidance in this vexing area, and to pass along some hints that are widely known among elite distance runners.

The first hint is to find a good sports medicine doctor and keep him or her; they're golden. Dr. Mirkin's book provides a list of these specialists by states.

The second hint is to learn the basics of self-help and to begin to treat injuries *when you first notice them.*

The third hint is to learn when you haven't succeeded with hint number two and you will therefore have to lay off training while you heal.

THE "ACHING EIGHT"

There are eight general injuries or groups of injuries. Most elite runners who have been competing for more than three or four years have experienced most or all of them. Some of the more hapless runners have been through them all several times. Strangely enough, they never seem to get used to it.

Perhaps the worst impact of repeated injuries is the all-important psychological one. It isn't much fun sitting in the stands watching the race go by while you adjust the ice pack on your favorite knee. Far better to get crafty about injuries and learn to overtreat them at the first sign of trouble. Your training diary can be helpful here. You should record every twinge or slight pain. Looking back over the course of a week or month, you can see the notations that were obviously just sore muscles or mysterious "pings" that disappeared in the night. You can also see those little notes which say: "Right ankle *still* sore," which translates into Trouble, with a capital T.

Following are the "Aching Eight" and my practical approach to dealing with them.

1. Achilles Tendon Problems

I believe most of these problems are caused by shoes with too much of a built-up heel. When I ran in college, we rarely, if ever (I don't remember once), had any achilles problems among our distance runners.

My theory is that too high a heel shortens calf muscles in the same way that women's high heels do. The calf becomes tight from exercise, exerts constant pressure on the achilles, which becomes irritated, which causes inflammation, which causes more irritation, and the beat goes on. Athletes who do nothing to alleviate the problem and who try to "run through" their achilles troubles will soon find themselves at a very painful standstill.

The first thing to do if you notice tenderness at the back of the heel where the tendon attaches, or higher up toward the calf, is *not* to abandon your padded-heel shoes. As a matter of fact, once you have actually begun to develop a problem, elevate the heel even more during running; this will take some of the pressure off the tendon. A simple heel pad made of Dr. Scholl's moleskin will do it. I've even heard of runner's making heel pads out of cardboard. Nearly anything will work.

The second thing is to take special care to warm up slowly to avoid straining the irritated tendon sheath even more. The runner should spend several minutes on an incline board stretching his calves out before beginning to jog. (Assuming, that is, that the problem hasn't already become acute. If it has, stretching may irritate the problem further.)

"RICE," the old reliable formula for all types of swelling injuries, comes into play here: Rest, Ice, Compression, Elevation. What I do for any of these injuries (including a sprained ankle) is simply to fill a Ziploc plastic bag with ice, with an Ace bandage wrap the bag of ice on the swelling, and then forget about it .When it gets so cold I can't stand it, I take it off for a while. But in general I just try to forget it and go about my business. If I have the time, or if it's convenient, I sit around and read or watch TV with the injured area elevated.

I have noticed that with achilles problems massage helps clear the area of swelling and the healing process in general.

In the long term, however, the answer is stretching the calf muscle. Once the injury is under control, the runner should begin wearing shoes with lower heels. Since many runners wear racing shoes which are much lower-heeled than many training shoes, they risk straining the achilles when they race.

As long as the runner begins to look after an achilles problem right away, he or she should be able to train through it. If the pain becomes worse or fails to respond to heel pads and stretching, the runner should stop training and seek a physician's help. It probably means the injury is no longer minor and the stretching and further training are merely exacerbating the difficulty.

2. Foot Problems in General

The foot, being the part of the body that actually hits the ground several thousand times during a run, naturally tends to take more than its share of abuse. But the foot is not important only because blisters hurt, but because any deviation in the foot-strike can cause reverberations throughout the runner's stride, and can thus lead to knee puffiness, hip pains, muscle strains, and the like.

Here is a rundown of the more common foot ailments and some suggestions for keeping them de-feeted.

Blisters: These are relatively simple to deal with, yet a surprising number of runners don't seem to know how to handle them. A new pair of shoes, for instance, will almost always cause problems in some place or another. Jog a short loop with them on before taking off across hill and dale. If you notice a "hot spot," a place that seems to be causing a little more irritation than you would like, smear some Vaseline directly on the part of the shoe that seems to be causing it. Also rub some on your foot where the irritation has made a red spot. If a blister has already formed, put some adhesive tape over the spot and then rub Vaseline on top of the tape.

The idea is that blisters are caused by friction, and the Vaseline eliminates that friction. Many runners make the mistake of trying to wear socks to avoid blisters. It doesn't work for the simple reason that the shoe will still irritate your foot at the hot spot, socks or no. Most distance runners do not wear socks to prevent blisters. Some have been known, however, to carry a little tube of Vaseline with them when trying out a new pair of training shoes.

If you happen to get a watery blister despite your precautions, you should sterilize a needle with a match, then lance the blister at the edge and allow the fluid to drain.

Some trainers in bygone days used to cut away the dead skin: a bad mistake, which can lead to infection. Better to leave the skin, coat it with Vaseline to eliminate further friction, then let nature take its course.

"Toenailitis": Distance runners seem to lose more than their share of toenails. And it can be painful.

Problems in this area are usually caused by shoes too tight or toenails too long. Keep them well-trimmed. If you still have problems, you might try "customizing" your shoes by cutting out the offending spots. Don't laugh. Some of the classiest runners in the world run around with shoes that look like mice got hold of them. Don't knock it until you try it.

Plantar Fasciitis: This is a sharp pain on the bottom of the foot caused by straining the fascia, which support the bottom of the foot. In runners it is often caused by pronation, or the turning inward of the ankle and the collapsing of the arch during foot-strike. Orthotics can be of some help with this problem, but it is not the kind of injury that can be run through. Once the fascia tears, it tears. Go see a doctor, then see about orthotics. The pain is usually right under the front of the heel, but it can radiate to any place along the fascia. You'll know it if you get it.

Plantar warts: You'll know these when you see them. Get them removed. They can spread and cause more problems. Since they are painful, they can throw your stride off and lead to compensation-type injuries. They occur on the bottom of the foot and look something like calluses. But they don't *feel* like calluses.

3. Knee Problems in General

I am of the opinion that many knee problems are actually caused by some difficulty in another area, generally the feet. Many elite runners have had the experience of a blister or sore toe causing an uneven stride, which later shows up as a puffy knee. The RICE formula is applicable to a puffy knee, but if the problem persists, the runner should see an orthopedic specialist familiar with sports injuries (preferably a running doctor) or a podiatrist (since a lot of these "transfer" problems radiate from the feet).

Chondromalacia, sometimes referred to as "runner's knee," is a common complaint in this area. It occurs when the kneecap rides unnaturally due to some anatomical problem, generally a difference in the strengths of the several muscles which hold it in line. The underside of the kneecap becomes soft and rough, and the pain can become quite debilitating. Surgery may be required in some severe cases, but the runner can head that off with the proper exercises. Cybex and Nautilus machines are helpful in this regard, but the runner can use simple leg weights to accomplish the same result. One simply sits on the edge of a table and extends the weighted foot straight out. After lowering it slowly, the process is repeated. This strengthens the muscles which hold the patella in place without placing great pressure directly on it.

The runner should probably check with a physician about any knee problem that persists for more than two days. Except for the occasional puffy knee caused by stepping in a soft spot or "landing funny" after striding off a curb, most knee problems do not go away by themselves if you keep on training.

4. Hamstring and Muscle Pulls and Strains

These injuries are more common to sprinters and lateral-movement-sports participants, but distance runners can also pull calf, hamstring, and other muscles. You will probably know it if you do it. A muscle strain is painful and it doesn't go away quickly. Occasionally, in the case of a severe pull, there may be internal hemorrhage and discoloration, as if one had been severely bruised.

Generally, however, the strain will be a sharp pain in the muscle which recurs every time the muscle contracts. Since this is an inflammatory injury, the RICE formula is applicable.

This is another injury that is very tricky to "run through." It may appear to the runner to have healed itself after a few days' layoff, but very often a return to full training will merely reinjure it.

I can speak from experience. It was a pulled muscle (caused by stepping in a small hole on a golf course) that caused me to miss the Olympic team in 1976. I had thought I had given it enough time to heal because it hadn't given me any trouble for several weeks prior to the AAU meet when it suddenly tore again during the last lap of the 5,000 meters.

In the case of a severe muscle pull, the runner should see a physician immediately. Anti-inflammatory drugs can help in some cases, and a sports-oriented doctor can often give you a realistic appraisal of your predicted "down time."

If the runner develops a slight strain (something sprinters sometimes call a "ping"), by careful warming up and special attention to stretching he or she may be able to train through it, so long as no fast running or hill training is undertaken. As a matter of fact, the increased circulation that comes with easy running can often be helpful in flushing out the fluid and dead cells that accompany an injury of this type.

5. Shin Splints

Caused by a tearing away of the muscle tissue that attaches to the front of the lower leg, this painful injury is often found in beginning runners but is not unknown among even elite athletes.

It is almost always caused by pounding on a hard surface. The best preventive is a pair of good, well-padded running shoes. Once the runner has shin splints, however, ice massage and special stretching exercises are recommended. One exercise is particularly helpful. In a kneeling position, the runner points his toes out behind him and gently sits back on his heels, pressing the tops of his feet toward the ground. This stretches the muscle tissue on the front of the lower leg and thus takes some of the pressure off the tear.

It may well be necessary to take time off from running to allow the shin splints to heal. If the case is severe enough, training will merely keep reinjuring the area. Athletes often report that the pain diminishes after warming up but then returns full force a few minutes after the completion of a workout.

Shin splints are extremely painful at times but are relatively harmless. An athlete may find him- or herself with an important meet at the end of the season and thus wish to continue training despite shin splints. There would appear to be no harm in this, particularly if more attention is paid to stretching and a gradual warm-up. Shin splints are almost never so debilitating as to affect competitive performance.

6. Stress Fractures

A stress fracture is a tiny crack in the bone caused by overuse. It is the same kind of thing that happens to a piece of metal which is bent back and forth until it finally breaks. Very often this kind of injury will occur in the small metatarsal bones of the foot, because they receive that same continuous bending motion thousands of times during the course of a long training session.

A stress fracture will generally not go away if training is continued at the same pace. It is possible to keep reinjuring the same area. If the reinjuring process goes on through several cycles, calcium deposits may complicate the matter. It is far better to allow healing to take place fully before trying to train, unless the runner is able to figure out the exact cause of the stress fracture and to counter it mechanically, perhaps through the use of orthotics.

A runner who suspects he or she has a stress fracture ought to see a physician. Although such hairline cracks often do not show up right away on X ray, an experienced sports physician can generally diagnose the problem. Once again, ice massage may be helpful in alleviating pain, but in the long run the athlete will need to let the healing process complete itself while engaging in alternative training programs.

7. Sciatica

This is a back problem suffered by even the elite runner. Caused by the crowding of nerves in the vertebrae, it can radiate pain anywhere along the base of the spine on down into the foot. A pain which shoots like a hot wire down your leg when you cough is a sure sign.

Runners who suffer from this problem have tried everything from rolfing to acupuncture. Elite runners desperate for relief from constant pain in training will even seek out psychics and other "nonscientific" sources of help. (John Walker claims a psychic healed a chronic knee problem of his.)

I have suffered from sciatica and the only real relief (I have tried acupressure, acupuncture, ultrasound, etc.) I found was from a chiropractor. My medical doctor friends can smirk all they want, but my back doesn't hurt like it used to.

In general chiropractors, although they may not be able to do everything they say they can, have a good reputation among top athletes.

8. Overtraining and Training-Related Illness

I lump a lot of these miseries together because, like stress injuries, they are generally caused by overuse, but overuse of the body as a whole, not a specific muscle or joint.

Overtraining is, to my way of thinking, the biggest medical problem incurred by talented runners who lack the experience or the discipline to cope with their own enthusiasm. I have often said that the biggest problem with talented young college runners is not in making them run hard enough, but in making them *stop* running when they should.

It is pretty easy to spot the symptoms of overtraining. The end result is a breakdown of some kind, usually a cold or flu, or perhaps a tendency to develop a string of nagging-type injuries. The overtrained athlete is, ironically, a sitting duck for diseases like mononucleosis because, though he or she is ostensibly one of the healthiest physical specimens around, overtraining lowers resistance to disease to levels the layman would scarcely believe.

An overtrained athlete will lose interest in training, have trouble eating or sleeping, find it difficult to study or work, and generally become an irritable person.

A general state of fatigue or sluggishness may envelop the runner, sometimes accompanied by a loss of weight and either constipation or diarrhea. Women may experience loss of menstruation.[61]

Experienced runners (who call overtraining "breaking down") are familiar enough with the symptoms and with their own bodies to be able gradually to work out of the situation. Novices should probably cut their training back to a few miles of jogging a day until the bounce returns to their legs.

Every effort should be made to eat properly during this general state of trauma, as the body will be fighting to replenish depleted nutrients and glycogen. Generally speaking, two or three days of light jogging will find the runner back ready to go.

Coaches should be particularly sensitive to overtraining symptoms in young runners and should take steps to bring them out of it. A young runner, if kept in the breakdown state for too long by a coach, will probably have a short running career.

WHAT TO DO IF ONE OF THE ACHING EIGHT GETS YOU

I have found that runners have a huge psychological problem if they get laid up by an injury. It's almost a guilty feeling, as if they are afraid of being accused of goldbricking instead of doing their mileage. This is perhaps caused by the fact that most runners' injuries are internal and don't require casts, slings, and other visible indicators of real hurt which skiers and football players can sport.

Another aspect of this brand of runner's insanity is caused by sheer nervous energy. Here you have an athlete with tremendous stores of energy, which is normally put to good use daily out on the roads or track, and all of a sudden there is no outlet for all that juice. No wonder runners think they're going crazy (a conclusion their spouses and loved ones would readily agree with—and would also claim that the disorder is apparently contagious, as everyone else in the household can be found climbing the walls as well).

For that reason, I heartily recommend that an injured runner take up some other form of aerobic exercise during the layoff period. The results in maintaining cardiovascular fitness should be obvious, but the psychological benefits are even more apparent. The runner should approach the alternative training with the same enthusiasm and drive with which he or she approaches the daily run. If the runner selects swimming, which is an excellent alternative, he or she should put the same patience and determination into covering as many yards as possible in a workout. The key factor is not the distance swum, but the elapsed time spent doing aerobic exercise. The runner will have difficulty at first venturing into this new medium. Twenty minutes spent swimming laps in a pool can seem like forever to a runner who thinks nothing of an hour and a half on the road. But with patience the runner will get more at ease in the water and soon recognize the same general feeling of well-being after a workout that running provides. In addition, swimming works upper-body muscle groups that don't get much attention from running, and such strength can pay off later during competition.

Another alternative is cycling, which works many of the same leg muscles (particularly the quadriceps), but without the traumatic pounding which produces so many running injuries. The same rules apply: at least 20 minutes for cardiovascular fitness; more later on as the runner becomes used to the new routine.

When Frank Shorter had his ankle operated on in 1978, he used a cycling machine for an hour a day to keep up muscle tone and cardiovascular fitness.

"I didn't even want to look out the window," he said grimly, after his two-month recuperation, "I just pushed it against the wall and started pumping." When he was able to begin jogging again, he was happy to find that he hadn't lost a great deal of his conditioning during the layoff.

Another alternative is the weight room. Because I believe that runners need upper-body strength, particularly in the shorter races, and I generally encourage weight lifting as a part of the runner's overall program, a forced layoff is a good time to lay a solid foundation of weight work.

When selecting an alternative form of training, it would be wise to check with a sports-oriented physician to make sure the alternative will be safe for the particular injury being nursed by the runner. For instance, a torn hamstring would not lend itself to certain types of weight training, or even to a vigorous flutter kick in the swimming pool.

THE FUTURE

Medical science and physiology, in cooperation with lay athletic experts, are making great strides in alleviating or mitigating the athlete's injury miseries. The Cybex machine, which can measure a muscle's strength and thus predict injuries caused by imbalances in the musculature, is a good example of such cooperation.

Even more fascinating is the Stimul One, an electrical stimulation machine developed by Dr. Yakov M. Kots of the Soviet Union. Although there are other machines which artificially induce muscle contractions by the use of electrical impulses, unlike them Dr. Kots's amazing machine is able to exercise muscles in that manner without any pain to the surrounding skin and other tissue.

The Stimul One has already shown remarkable results in helping athletes treat injuries, and even in exercising healthy athletes' muscles to develop undreamed-of strength (the

Russians claim the machine added an average of an incredible four inches to the jumping ability of their national volleyball team!). But perhaps the most fascinating prospects for this machine which trains muscles with no effort on the part of the owner of those muscles lie in its humanitarian possibilities.

Says Dr. Kots:

> The real value of my machine will come with this machine's application for mass medicine, particularly in the cases of people who have a hard time getting their muscles back in shape after an accident. This is particularly true of older people, who often are laid up for weeks after they slip, fall and break a bone.
>
> Think of the handicapped, and the totally paralyzed. We can't offer them a cure, of course, but perhaps, particularly with transmitters, we can keep some tone in their muscles so they can at least manage some of the bodily functions on their own.[62]

In December 1977, Kots took his remarkable Stimul One to Canada and proceeded to amaze a group of Canadian scientists and doctors with it. A group of fifteen student athletes had muscle biopsies performed before and after a ten-day regimen in which they had their thigh muscles stimulated with the machine.

Said Dr. Bert Taylor, Canada's foremost sports medicine expert: "There is no doubt that there were changes in the muscle fibers in just ten days. There is just nothing in my experience in biochemistry that allows me to explain why that happened. To the best of my knowledge it shouldn't have happened."[63]

Is it any wonder that exercise physiologists are now talking about the day when citizens of a future world will sit down in their Stimul One reclining chairs and set the dial for whatever kind of exercise program they desire?

And if the future really holds such wonders in store, is the ancient, idealized image of the athlete, an image which has somehow survived from the age of Pericles to the modern era, rapidly becoming obsolete? Will the headless Discobolus of Grecian times be replaced by the soulless cyborg of the twenty-first century?

Chapter Six

The Race

All the hours spent on the track doing intervals, all the miles piled up on the roads and cross-country courses are not worth a damn if the runner cannot put it all together on the day of a race.

As I have mentioned before, there are a number of unfortunate individuals who seemingly are unbeatable except that they can't race. They apparently have the necessary physical equipment, they do incredible workouts, they seem to have everything going for them, but they just can't seem to do the right thing in a racing situation. They inevitably turn in their best times against poor competition, when they simply run away from the pack and coast in by a wide margin: a fast frog in a slow puddle.

I have pondered long and hard to pinpoint the reason for the apparent inability of some runners to race well. I have concluded that the skill of running races is entirely separate and apart from the skill and dedication needed to do the necessary training to run well.

I have also discussed this with athletes from other sports, and they all know some performers in their sports as well who are great in practice and all but useless when it counts. Others, of course, show little on the practice field yet shine with great consistency when the pressure is on.

The conclusion is inescapable: The ability to run a race is an art unto itself. All you have to do to convince yourself of that is to watch some gifted and experienced runner winning a race that by all rights he should not win. I know. I have won such races myself.

Naturally, skill at strategy and tactics pays off more readily in track races that it does on the roads, but even that may be changing. Frank Shorter told me he thought the Olympic marathon was becoming exactly like a track race:

> Think of it. Everyone knows who to watch for, just like in a track event. You all go out together, the front pack forms, people try to surge and break away. Some go with them, others drop back. Very late in the race, those who are still in it will make their moves.
>
> The race may be run outside the stadium, but it is a track race nonetheless.

Thus having the physical attributes of a great endurance athlete and doing the incredible amounts of hard work necessary to perfect those attributes are only two parts of a three-part formula. The last part is the ability to prepare for and run the race itself. There is no doubt in my mind that many races are lost by superior athletes who fritter away their energy or who psych themselves out of a race in the two or three days prior to a major competition.

Two factors must be considered: proper handling of the details in the 48 hours prior to competition (i.e., planning out meals, getting the proper rest, avoiding fretting, etc.) and proper execution during the race itself. The first factor is sometimes more important than the second.

THE PRERACE FRITTERS

Adrenaline and nervous energy are nothing to be feared. They are, in fact, a necessary ingredient in an outstanding athletic performance. Every athlete knows the importance of "getting psyched up."

But that adrenaline and those butterflies doing figure eights in your stomach will only be helpful if they make themselves felt only in the final minutes before the race begins. It is not only unhelpful, but downright counterproductive to get your mind and heart racing two days or even two hours before the start of competition. If the runner thinks of nothing but the race for the entire week before the competition, if he or she is unable to get his proper rest during that all-important rest period, then he or she might well find him- or herself on the starting line in a state approaching exhaustion (mental if not physical).

What can be done about the "prerace fritters"?

The answer: *Use, Don't Abuse, That Adrenaline.*

The mind must be trained in much the same way as the body. Many younger athletes feel guilty if they are not thinking about their race the night before the competition. The result of such total attention just prior to competition is the "fritters." It can sometimes mean the difference between winning and losing, because every time a shot of adrenaline enters the system, it causes the body to go into a stressful "fight or flight" mode. The athlete who has cut back on training during the final days before competition is the last person in the world who needs extra adrenaline making him or her agitated and unable to sleep or to digest food.

Coaches sometimes smile to each other about how worked up their kids get before competition. But an athlete who has to throw up before every game or race is an athlete who hasn't learned to control his or her own body; the athlete may well be an outstanding performer, but who knows how much better he or she could be if all that nervous energy were brought to bear on opponents rather than the athlete's digestive tract?

What is the secret? I try to turn off all thoughts of a race in the final days before competing. I learned to do it early in my racing career and I have never doubted that it was the best way to cope with the prerace fritters.

It is sometimes not easy to do, but young athletes should begin teaching themselves that kind of control. It is far more difficult to learn later on, when there is greater pressure because more attention is focused on the race.

I found it particularly necessary to employ such control in 1969, when I ran several extremely pressure-filled mile races against Jim Ryun. The runner appreciates the value of mind control in such situations when the ballyhoo runs wild. During the final days before that all-important competition—whether it's the Olympic finals or your college conference meet—though the race should be in the back of your mind, you should always keep your mind on the present—the book you're reading, the movie you just saw, the conversation you're having with your girl friend, what you're going to have for dinner, etc. There will be time to think of the race, and that time will be during the hour you do your warm-up.

That hour is the first time I allow the adrenaline to start flowing. And then I keep it flowing all the way through to the finish line.

FEAR AND LOATHING ON THE RACING TRAIL

Runners who hope to compete successfully also have to learn to cope with prerace fear. All runners go through the same mixture of agony and fear just prior to important races, but few have really analyzed what they are afraid of.

Generally speaking, they are afraid that when they get to the crucial point of the race and the discomfort (to some, "pain") is at its peak, they might back off the pace and let themselves down by not giving their maximum effort.

This fear can be dealt with only through experience. The runner who has put in hundreds of tough miles of overdistance and interval work will learn to control his or her adrenaline and put forth a maximum effort nearly every time he or she sets foot on the starting line (assuming the runner doesn't "overcompete"). Again, it is a matter of mind control. The runner knows that the stress to be faced in a race will be tough, but he or she also knows that it is surely no worse than most of the grueling interval workouts or even some of the faster overdistance runs.

After properly handling the prerace fritters successfully several times, the runner should gain confidence that the stress of the race will be taken in stride. When that confidence is developed, the runner will then be able to concentrate more on the competition, the pace of the race, important weather factors, and the like, and less on introspective fears.

There *will* be stress and discomfort, but the runner has been properly trained to handle it. The stress is familiar to the trained athlete, and thus it holds—or should hold—no true terror. The runner knows that there will come a time in every race when he or she wants to quit, but he or she also knows that that barrier can be overcome and later on it will seem like a ridiculous thought to have entertained.

THE POWER OF POSITIVE DAYDREAMING

The first race every champion runner ever won was in a daydream (or perhaps in a normal nighttime dream).

In order to program ourselves for success in any difficult endeavor, we must first be able to picture ourselves actually succeeding in that endeavor.

Dick Fosbury, the winner of the high jump in the 1968 Olympics in Mexico City, used to stand in front of the bar before his jumps and just imagine himself floating over the height. Most high jumpers and pole vaulters go through similar rituals before their leaps.

It is a process I try to use in everyday life. If you want to win the Boston Marathon, you must first try to imagine yourself neck and neck with Bill Rodgers with 100 yards to go. Rodgers admits that he himself invents imaginary competitors to run against. He even gives them silly nicknames to make them more real. Psyching yourself to stay on top is just as important as psyching yourself to get there.

You must be able to imagine yourself getting into the race, feeling good, feeling comfortable with the pace, reaching down for a kick, passing runners, sprinting to the tape, and then hitting it first.

If you want to be a champion, you will have to win every race in your mind a hundred times before you win it in real life that last time. You will see yourself in that race on your morning runs, in your afternoon overdistance, and especially in your intervals on the track.

You will need to learn, as I have learned from sports, that the mind is an incredibly important factor in athletic success. It is probably *the* most important single factor because, without it, the most naturally talented athlete in the world will achieve little more than trivial local recognition. The athletes who truly "make it," the Olympic contenders, the national champions, the world record holders, are mentally some of the toughest people in the world.

No one is born with that kind of toughness, and it doesn't come overnight. You must develop it, cultivate it, cherish it.

Without it you will never wear the laurel wreath.

TRAINING DURING THE RACING SEASON

The problem with many training programs is that they show you how to get into shape for the racing season, then they leave you hanging, saying something like: "Now you're ready to race. Go to it."

That is a problem even many elite runners have after they have attained racing fitness: What do I do now?

If you have run a Personal Record in April, you are immediately faced with a question: How do I maintain this shape through July?

How do I handle those two days prior to a big race, cope with the travel problems, the Big Mac nutrition problems, the strange environment of the competition site?

Jumbo Elliot, my coach at Villanova, was a master at handling his runners at such crucial competitive times.

His first rule was: "After you start hard racing, hard training will get you nowhere."

You can expect only one primary reaction from your body at any given time. Either you can be stressing it in training so that it will be stronger later in a race, or you can be resting it to be ready for that race. You can't expect your body to give you both reactions at the same time. Therefore, once you start racing, don't attempt to keep training at a high level.

Secondly, Jumbo used to say: "Live like a clock." That simply meant that once the stress of training was removed, the runner should still keep his or her same basic schedule in order not to confuse the body's time clock. Thus, even though you may not need to rise and run your normal five or six miles in the morning, you may still need to go out and jog two miles, just to stay on a similar schedule. Don't sleep 12 hours one night, then six the next. Your body will be set in a groove from your rigorous training schedule over all those months; don't blow it during the crucial weeks of competition. Even if you are just going through the motions, you should still keep to your schedule. This is especially important when traveling and changing time zones. A light jog after arriving at your destination will help to reorient you. It will relax you, get you back in "the groove," help you to sleep.

The racing season is a time when many runners tend to overeat. Jumbo's solution to that was simply to give his runners a meal allowance. Knowing that college students would spend the money in a miserly fashion and pocket the difference, Jumbo was avoiding the overstuffing that would result from going to a restaurant and having him say: "Okay boys, six dollars and fifty cents is the limit, eat up!" That would ensure that every one of us would get $6.47 worth of food.

I try to watch my diet at this important time when my lack of mileage would make putting on weight a real possibility. I also like to avoid eating for five or six hours before a major race. That leaves me a little hungry, grouchy, and perhaps more aggressive. There are other runners who like to have something for their stomachs to work on, however, so that is something each individual has to work out on a trial-and-error basis.

As far as training during the competitive season goes, the watchword is: "Light and fast. Plenty of rest."

Here is a sample workout week for the racing season:

Monday	A.M.	3 miles easy
	P.M.	12 × 220 easy
Tuesday	A.M.	3 miles easy
	P.M.	8 miles overdistance easy
Wednesday	A.M.	3 miles easy
	P.M.	8 × 440 medium intensity
Thursday		8 miles easy

Friday	6 miles easy
Saturday	RACE
Sunday	10 to 15 miles, easy jog, to recover

Once in the racing phase, the runner must constantly be evaluating his or her condition. He or she should not panic if the first several races don't astonish the world. If the training has been done properly, the runner will come around with the proper sharpening and rest. The runner, above all, shouldn't fall into the trap of trying to continue working hard in training because his or her racing doesn't meet expectations right away.

As a general rule, if you run a race and the early pace seems too fast, but you have a good kick, you probably have done sufficient aerobic overdistance, and what you really need is more interval work so that your anaerobic pathways start contributing to the pace work.

If, on the other hand, you feel great throughout the race but just can't seem to kick at the end, ironically you probably need more aerobic conditioning. It might well be that you are either overraced or that you have used up your "peak" and need to go back and start building the base again.

That inability to dredge up a kick in a race that otherwise went well is a sure sign to me that I have run out my peak and need to go home to start my training process all over again.

STRATEGY FOR ROAD RACING

Strategy and tactics are both military words used to describe the process of attempting to outmaneuver or outwit an opponent.

The first step in that process is to evaluate the weapons you have in your own arsenal. Every runner has individual strengths and weaknesses, and the very best runners are well aware of both and try to use that knowledge to their own advantage.

It is not wise to attempt to decide your strengths and weaknesses too early in your running career. Many athletes in their first year or two of competition decide that they do not have a kick or that they are not very good on hills. I would advise against making such decisions until the runner is thoroughly tested.

For example, a runner may very well develop a capacity for speed that neither he nor his coach suspected was there. When Jim Ryun first ran cross-country at Wichita High School, he never suspected that he would later develop the kind of speed many quarter-milers in his state would envy. He was actually able to run under 47 seconds for a quarter on the mile relay team.

Once the runner has some racing experience, he or she should then begin to evaluate what there is at his or her disposal to throw against the opposition. The runner will have to ask him- or herself many questions, some of them detailed. For instance, a runner may recognize that he or she has a good kick, but *what* kind of kick?

Even some well-read track fans are unaware that some kickers are better with a long, sustained sprint (I fall into that category), whereas others are all but unbeatable in the last 100 or the last 50 yards.

Some runners might have fairly good leg speed, but for some reason always get overhauled at the end of big races. For them, a strong surging technique might be their best weapon, using both their strength *and* speed to break a race wide open in the middle when everyone else is just angling for position.

There are many other questions: Do you run up hills well? Can you use such an advantage to "break" opponents? Do you have a nice long flowing stride you can use to get away from the pack going *down* hills? Are you mentally strong enough to go to the front and try to win the race by running away from all competition?

It is helpful indeed to have a coach or perhaps an experienced runner for a mentor in evaluating your talents as compared to other runners he or she has seen in action.

I was fortunate early in my running career to have had a coach who quickly recognized that although I could run the last 400 meters of a race very quickly, my greatest speed was during the first 300 meters of that kick, and that I was *not* an outstanding sprinter in the last 100 meters or so. Therefore, we adjusted my training to make sure that, with 100 meters to go, I had already made my move and had a four- or five-yard cushion.

Only through experience can a runner learn these things or be taught them. Only after assessing personal strengths and weaknesses, and then having the willpower to take advantage of that knowledge in training and racing, will the runner understand how important his or her intelligence is in deciding the outcome of a race.

I like to remind people that the first four-minute mile was run by a very intelligent, very precise English doctor named Roger Bannister, who planned every yard of his attack on the four-minute barrier. It was *not* run by John Landy, who most experts agree was on paper the superior runner, and who clearly was doing more intense training than Bannister at the same time.

Let's look at the situation 98 percent of all runners face. Most runners who line up for a race are not thinking of winning the race. In the beginning they are thinking of running the best race they can run at the moment, given their physical condition.

Most of us are satisfied if we feel we have run up to our potential. So the first thing you must do is set a realistic yet challenging goal, keeping in mind what your training and previous racing experience tell you about your fitness.

Then divide the race up into segments. In a mile, the race

is divided into four equal quarter-miles; in a 10,000-meter race, into six separate miles with an extra 385 yards tacked onto the end.

Physiologically there are only three ways to expend your energy to meet your goal. The first is to go out hard and fast and then try to hang on until the finish line. This is undoubtedly the most painful way to run, as it incurs an oxygen debt early and forces the runner to endure such a condition throughout the race.

The second method is to judge the pace evenly and try to run each segment of the race as fast as every other segment.

The third method is to run a fairly even pace for 80 percent of the race and finish with a kick at the end. Since the very first footrace thousands of years ago, people have experimented with these three different styles, trying to decide which was the most efficient.

In the nineteenth century Walter George thought he could set world records by running much faster during the first half of a race, when he was still "fresh." He did in fact set records in that manner. In the late 1960s and early 1970s, most runners tried to use the third strategy. When, however, the African runners (notably Kip Keino and Filbert Bayi) appeared on the scene during those years, the idea of front-running again became popular.

Nowadays the physiologists tell us that the best way to produce a fast time from a scientific point of view is to run most of the race at a steady, even pace, and then to kick at the end.

Each runner will have to experiment with those three approaches to racing to find which is best suited to him or her. If you decide that you are truly bold and strong you might want to try the latest, and most difficult, racing strategy: surging. My own recommendation is that unless you have trained to handle the quick lactic-acid buildup which surging produces in the middle of a race, you had best leave that method to the more experienced runners. A high school athlete will more likely find himself "surging" himself right out of a race rather than doing the opposition any real damage.

What does the runner think about during the long middle miles of a road race?

This is a question that often divides the racers from the joggers. Psychological studies have shown that world-class runners spend all of their time, even in marathon races, thinking about the race itself, monitoring their position in the race, their relative fatigue, their stride, rhythm, and so on. Nonelite runners, on the other hand, reported thinking of anything *but* the race.[64]

Therein lies a big difference. The elite runner is able to concentrate on the race, even over 26-plus miles, whereas the less competitive runner seeks to escape the discomfort of the race. Almost all runners daydream during overdistance training, but racing is serious business to them.

Therefore, the more time you spend during the race thinking about the race, the more competitive you are becoming as a runner.

The intense concentration of a Bill Rodgers or a Frank Shorter during a marathon is no less than that of a Lee Trevino or a Jack Nicklaus bending over a 20-foot putt which may make him several hundred thousand dollars.

The best strategy a runner can have in a road race is to set a realistic time goal, to run as even a pace as possible in order to stay on schedule for that goal, and then, with 25 percent of the race remaining, to pick a runner somewhere ahead and do everything short of mayhem to beat that runner to the finish line. (The runner one picks does not, of course, have to be the person at the front of the pack.) You may not always do it, but when you do, you'll know what it feels like to win a race.

STRATEGY FOR TRACK RACING

I have always been fascinated with tactics in track races. On the 400-meter oval, the strongest and best-conditioned athlete does not always win. As a matter of fact, I would venture to say that generally speaking the smartest runner gets to the tape first in trackdom.

The track runner, as opposed to the road racer, must always be thinking of his or her position relative to the other athletes in the race. No matter how much of a kick you have left, you cannot win a race in the home stretch if there are three runners in front of you, or if you have to swing out into the fifth lane coming around the last turn because you got boxed in. On the track, all it takes is one runner in front of you and one runner on your right shoulder; unless you feel like going out the back door, you have been boxed in. A mile, a 5,000-meter, or a 10,000-meter race thus becomes a tactical chess game in which the runner must make split-second decisions as to what to do and what the opposition will probably do.

Many runners never quite learn the skill (nerve?) it takes to run in a pack. That means they are forced either to run from the front or else trail far off the pace.

When the gun goes off you can do one of three things: try to hold the lead, fight for position in the middle of the pack, or drop to the back. All three have drawbacks and advantages.

Taking the lead has these advantages: (1) You can avoid the inevitable jostling for position going around the first turn; (2) You can run at your own pace (so long as it is fast enough to avoid being passed immediately); (3) You will be assured of running close to the inside of the track and therefore of covering the shortest distance around the curve;

and (4) Your parents, friends, or spouse can get good pictures of you leading the race.

The disadvantages are these: (1) If it is windy, you're the sucker making it easier for everyone else; (2) You can't see what the other runners are up to; (3) You often will be forced to continue to lead or take a chance on being boxed in during the later stages.

This is a good point to mention the First Commandment of Track Racing: When thou art passed by a runner, move to his or her outside shoulder. Why? Because once you are passed and there is a runner in front of you, you are vulnerable to the box. All that is necessary is another runner to come up to *your* outside shoulder and the box is complete. Let's repeat that: When you are passed, immediately move to the outside shoulder of the runner who just passed you. You don't have to pass him back, just hang there off his shoulder. You will have to run a little farther around the curves but it's a lot better than trying to run out of a box.

Why does anyone try to lead the whole race? Front-runners feel their chances of success lie in running away from the kickers in the field. They feel that a fast pace is the only chance they have of doing well in the race if there are competitors present who can surely outsprint them. Most front-runners are very tough mentally and are very experienced. It is not a technique recommended for the novice runner.

Most runners take the middle course and go for the center of the pack. Such a tactic has these advantages: (1) You can tuck yourself into the group and forget about the pace because you're just along for the ride; (2) You will be sheltered from the wind and will get the benefit of the aerodynamic "drafting" of the runners in front who break a slight pathway through the air for you; (3) You can keep good tabs on just about everyone in the race and if you decide to make a move, you will have the advantage of surprise and may get past the leaders before they can react; (4) You will have more choice in the pace you run because you can either stay with the leaders or drop back if you feel the pace is too fast; and (5) You won't use extra energy in a nervous rush during the first 200 yards, as sometimes happens to the early leader.

There are, of course, disadvantages: (1) You may be jostled by other runners; (2) The leader may surge and catch you "sleeping at the switch" or else boxed in.

Finally, you can run from the back of the pack. The advantages are: (1) You avoid the jostling of the pack; (2) You can run your own pace; (3) You can keep good tabs on the race; (4) You can wait until the field settles down and then begin picking your way up through the runners when they have become strung out; and (5) You can be assured that you won't kick too early because you can see the entire field. If anyone surprises anyone, it will be you doing the honors.

The disadvantages of running from the back are considerable: (1) If the pace is very slow, the runners may bunch up in a pack, blocking even the fourth and fifth lanes, making passing difficult; (2) You will have to pass everyone in the race at least once if you want to win, using extra energy to do so; (3) You may lose contact with the leaders and feel as though you are running on your own, a difficult psychological obstacle because it is similar to running from the front—you are in effect leading your own race.

Through experience you will be able to see the different situations shaping up as the race progresses. There aren't an infinite number of situations, just a dozen or so, but being able to react to them when the body is weary and the mind preoccupied is rather more challenging than anything available on the chessboard.

If you are a good finisher and you decide to use your kick to win, decide in advance where you will make your move. Of course, you can always revise your plan if you have to, but you should try to stick to it no matter how difficult it may seem at the time. The satisfaction you will get from properly executing your race plan is guaranteed to repay the effort. But if you really must revise your plan, then you are the final judge of that. For instance, if the early pace has been much faster than you expected, and you find yourself just barely hanging on to the leaders, you may figure that you can't sustain as long a kick as you had previously counted on. You might then decide to attack over the last 100 yards, instead of the last 300. That is an example of a mid-race revision which could help you win the race.

If you are a front-runner and have properly executed your race plan, don't despair if you are passed toward the end of the race. Your tactic may have worked after all. Perhaps you really have run the legs off the kickers and they themselves have become vulnerable to a fast finish by a stronger runner, namely you. Thus you should follow closely and attempt to retake the lead when you see your opportunity.

Very often it is not the first kicker to make a move who ends up winning the race, but the one who picks the exact right moment to surprise everyone, including his or her fellow kickers.

No matter what strategy you use, whether you run from the front, middle, or back of the pack, whether you set the pace or save your kick, you should remember a rule observed by every great runner I have ever known or heard of: Never stop racing until you have crossed the finish line. Not a lap before, not a foot before, not an inch before.

You have trained too hard to give anyone back even a millimeter of the ground you have covered.

If you have followed the training advice and the schedules set forth in this book, if you have taken good care of yourself and haven't been unduly plagued by injury or illness, if you have studied some of the history of distance running and the racing tactics described in this book, then you are as well prepared to run races as any novice could be.

The only thing left for you to do is race, and you should understand by this time that a footrace is one of those activities undertaken by human beings which *must* be undertaken alone.

If you have prepared well, win or lose, you cannot help but be proud of yourself, for, as Rudyard Kipling wrote in 1892:

> If you can fill the unforgiving minute
> With sixty seconds' worth of distance run—
> Yours is the Earth and everything that's in it . . .

Good luck.

NOTES

1. Jack Daniels, et al., *Conditioning for Distance Runners*, John Wiley & Son, N.Y. 1978.
2. Kenny Moore, "Watching Their Steps," *Sports Illustrated*, May 3, 1973, p. 84.
3. Moore, op cit., p. 83. The reason that results are sometimes confusing is that occasionally the laboratory findings simply don't match the runner's racing history. Marathoner Don Kardong, not known for his sprint but highly regarded for his ability to hold a fast pace, had only 53 percent slow-twitch cells. But there's always a hedge: "his slow fibers were large," reported Dr. Costill, who helped coordinate the tests.
4. John L. Parker, "Olympic Forum," *Runner's World*, November, 1972.
5. Dr. David L. Costill, *A Scientific Approach to Distance Running*, Tafnews Press, 1979, p. 60.
6. Ibid., p. 32.
7. Daniels, p. 13.
8. Ibid., p. 6.
9. Arthur Lydiard and Garth Gilmour, *Running the Lydiard Way*, World Publications, 1978, p. 16.
10. Daniels, p. 6.
11. Costill, p. 79.
12. Ibid., p 18.

13. Daniels, p. 7.
14. Costill, p. 25.
15. Ibid., p. 11.
16. Ibid, p. 79.
17. Compare, for instance, Henderson's incorrect but common usage in *Jog, Run, Race*, World Publications, 1977, p. 55, with Fred Wilt, *Run, Run, Run,* Tafnews Press 1964, p. 201.
18. Wilt, p. 197.
19. Lydiard, p. 91.
20. Costill, p. 94.
21. Ron Clarke and Garth Gilmour, *The Lonely Breed*, Pelham Books, 1967.
22. Sam Merrill, "Zatopek: Then and Now," *The Runner*, December 1979, p. 42.
23. Roger Bannister, *The Four Minute Mile*, Dodd, Mead & Co., 1966, N.Y.
24. Ibid., p. 200.
25. Clarke, p. 111.
26. American runners, who must peak for our Olympic trials in June, have a difficult time maintaining that edge until the end of August, when they will need to run their ultimate race. Other countries select their Olympic athletes on the basis of past performances. While this allows for some pretty insidious politicking, it does allow their athletes to avoid the "double peak" problem. It also gives injured athletes a chance to heal before the games, something the United States should consider.
27. Peter Snell and Garth Gilmour, *No Bugles, No Drums*, Minerva, 1965, p. 39.
28. Ron Clarke and Alan Trengove, *The Unforgiving Minute*, Pelham Books, 1966.
29. Lydiard, p. 127.
30. George Gandy, "Blueprinting the Perfect Runner," *Runner's World*, May 1980, p. 69.
31. It has been demonstrated that elite runners have a much better insight into their own fatigue during a treadmill exhaustion run than do even good college runners. See Moore, p. 90.
32. "Running Out of Romance," *Parade Magazine*, March 16, 1980.
33. John L. Parker, "Professor Fast Food," *Tropic Magazine*, October 1, 1978, p. 14.
34. A. S. Ushakov, et al., *Aviation, Space and Environmental Medicine*, 49:1184-1187, October 1978; reported in *1979 Year Book of Sports Medicine*, Year Book Medical Publishers, 1979, p. 139.
35. David Costill, unpublished interview with author, February, 1980.
36. Ed Gilbert, *The Miracle Machine*, Dodd, Mead, 1980, p. 186.
37. Dr. Peter Hanson and Dr. David Costill, quoted by Bill Hauda in *National Joggers' Association Newsletter*, Spring, 1980, p. 22.

38. Ibid.
39. Costill, pp. 91-92.
40. Helen Lane and James Cerda, *Journal of American Dietary Association*, 73:64-65, July, 1978; reported in *1979 Year Book of Sports Medicine*, p. 140.
41. Costill, p. 120.
42. Ibid., p. 22.
43. Dr. Costill recently said that the use of caffeine is one of the training techniques that seems to have widely varying affects, depending upon the individual. The theory is basically that caffeine permits the free fatty acids in the system to be used more quickly for energy. I have found that taking 100 milligrams of caffeine before a 20-mile run has been very helpful. Again, this is entirely subjective.

    Dr. Costill points out that taking caffeine in the form of several cups of coffee can have undesirable side effects, such as a need to urinate or defecate while running; I use it in tablet form. There are researchers who claim that caffeine's drawbacks outweigh its advantages, but once again these "experts" generally have no experience with highly trained athletes and are generally ignored by runners who put more faith in their own analyses.

    I make no moral judgment on the use of a chemical like caffeine. I do not drink more than one cup of coffee a day; however, I will probably use caffeine on my weekly 20-mile run in the future.
44. C. V. Gisolfi, et al., *Annals of the New York Academy of Sciences*, 301:139-150, 1977; reported in *1979 Year Book of Sports Medicine*, p. 216. There is little informed dissent from this statement: ". . . the only serious threat to the physical well-being of a marathon runner is the possibility of a fatal thermal injury, or heat stroke. . . ."
45. Costill, pp. 94–95.
46. Ibid., p. 95. The physiological changes in the body after months of altitude training are fairly well documented now. The most common effect is the marked rise in the hemoglobin count in the blood, which means that the oxygen-carrying capacity of the blood is increased. In dealing with this adaptation, we should perhaps pay attention to the conclusions of Dr. Jack Daniels, currently the women's track coach at the University of Texas. This excellent exercise researcher was instrumental in preparing our U.S. Olympic team for the 1968 games in the high altitude of Mexico City. From his vast experience on the subject, Dr. Daniels now concludes that altitude training does not necessarily increase a runner's chances at sea level, but that it certainly is of great benefit to a runner competing at altitude. This is in accord with my impression that training at altitude does not seem to help a world-class athlete improve his or her best times.

    Dr. Daniels does feel that non-world-class runners can be trained more rapidly at altitude, simply because the thinner air makes workouts more difficult.

Some runners who believe in the "Altitude Secret" like to point to the many overnight success stories of runners who move to places like Boulder, Colorado, and quickly become elite runners. This can be explained by other factors besides altitude. Generally such runners, by moving to a "running mecca," make a full-time commitment to running which they may not have made before. Further, in such locales there is usually a good deal more impetus, in the form of peer pressure as well as peer encouragement, to train harder. The same thing happens in Gainesville, Florida, which boasts an altitude of about three feet.

47. Moore, p. 82.
48. B. Ekblom and B. Gullbring, *Journal of Applied Physiology*, 33:175-180, 1972. In this, the most well-known of the early papers on the subject, the claim was made that blood reinfusion could demonstrably improve performance. That claim has been endlessly debated.
49. Costill, p. 78.
50. M. Williams, et al., *Medicine and Science in Sports*, 10:113-118, Summer, 1978; reported in *1979 Year Book of Sports Medicine*, p. 167.
51. Moore, p. 84.
52. Dr. Gabe Mirkin and Marshall Hoffman, *The Sportsmedicine Book*, Little, Brown and Company, 1978, p. 84.
53. Ekblom and Gulbring, R. Robertson, et al. and F. J. Buick, et al., *Medicine and Science in Sports*, 10:49, 1978.
54. Costill, p. 78; Williams, p. 167.
55. See, for instance, Gilbert's report (p. 186) of poor nutrition among highly trained elite Canadian athletes. I have long agreed that runners with difficult training schedules, not to mention financial problems, run the risk of becoming physically worn down by poor eating habits.
56. Lydiard, p. 37.
57. Snell, p. 120.
58. Gilbert, p. 186.
59. Lydiard, p. 49.
60. Mirkin, p. 130.
61. Ibid., p. 33.
62. Gilbert, p. 182.
63. Ibid.
64. Moore, p. 89.